THINGS TO DO IN
SAVANNAH
BEFORE YOU
DIE

EW!

ALL NEW!

100
THINGS TO DO IN
SAVANNAH
BEFORE YOU
DIE

• •

LYNN AND CELE SELDON

REEDY PRESS

Library of Congress Control Number: 2019952603

ISBN: 9781681062501

Design by Jill Halpin

Photos by author unless otherwise noted.

Printed in the United States of America
20 21 22 23 24   5 4 3 2 1

Please note that websites, phone numbers, addresses, and company names are subject to change or cancellation. We did our best to relay the most accurate information available, but due to circumstances beyond our control, please do not hold us liable for misinformation. When exploring new destinations, please do your homework before you go.

DEDICATION

To the people and places of Savannah
and all of the Peach State.

CONTENTS

• •

• •

Culture and History

Mercer-Williams House
Photo courtesy of visitsavannah.com

ACKNOWLEDGMENTS

When Savannah friends and veteran visitors learned about *100 Things to Do in Savannah Before You Die*, ideas for what to include came pouring into our inboxes and phones. We could not have written this book without the help of dozens of people. You know who you are. Thank you!

Everyone we contacted at restaurants, hotels, attractions, shops, and elsewhere was as helpful and charming as possible—we expected nothing less in "The Hostess City." This book serves as a long thank-you note to all of them and to everyone who makes visiting or living in Savannah one of the world's most hospitable experiences.

Much of this book was written in beloved Pat Conroy's home office overlooking a low-country creek, including several entries emanating from Pat's many visits to Savannah with his sister Kathy decades ago. Thanks and great love to Cassandra King Conroy for once again sharing her home and Pat's inspiring office with us.

We'd also especially like to thank Joe Marinelli, Erica Backus, and the rest of the incredible team at Visit Savannah. For more than two decades, dozens of visits, and hundreds of meals, they have made researching and writing stories—and now a book—like writing a love letter to a city and her people.

• •

PREFACE

We think that it will be obvious throughout this book that we love Savannah. From world-class culinary experiences and varied accommodations options to history, architecture, glorious squares, the great outdoors, friendly locals, and lots more, there's simply no other city in the world quite like Savannah.

First-time and veteran visitors, as well as residents exploring their own city, should head to the main MLK Visitor Information Center, located in the old train station at 301 Martin Luther King Jr. Blvd., to gather brochures and information, purchase tour and attraction tickets, and ask questions of the hospitable staff members. There are also several other helpful visitor centers in the area, including the Savannah Area Chamber of Commerce/Visit Savannah (101 E Bay St.), River Street Visitor Information Center (1 W River St.), Georgia Visitors Center–Savannah (mile marker 111 on Interstate 95 South), Savannah Airport Visitor Center (400 Airways Ave., inside the terminal), and Tybee Island Visitor Center (Campbell Ave. and Hwy 80). Visit Tybee also welcomes visitors at the Visit Tybee Visitor Information Center (802 1st St., Tybee Island).

Although much of Savannah is attractively walkable, Chatham Area Transit (CAT) provides an easy and affordable way to maneuver around much of Savannah without a car. Their bus service features twenty routes, including "Airport Express" service. They also offer frequent and free downtown shuttle service called the dot, which connects many downtown squares and sites. CAT operates the free Savannah Belles

• •

Ferry as well, which links River Street and Hutchinson Island, across the Savannah River.

With so many unique things to see and do, we had a difficult time narrowing down our list of "100 Things" for Savannah. We'd love to hear about your experiences with our choices and learn other "100 Things" possibilities. Find us on Facebook, Twitter, and Instagram @SeldonInk and tag your own #100ThingsSavannah adventures.

—Lynn and Cele Seldon

Leopold's Ice Cream Cone
Photo courtesy visitsavannah.com

FOOD AND DRINK

TAKE A BITE OUT OF SAVANNAH
AT THE SAVANNAH FOOD & WINE FESTIVAL

One of the tastiest and most efficient ways to take a bite out of the Savannah food and drink scene is the seven-day Savannah Food & Wine Festival in early November. Exuding Southern taste and hospitality and Savannah style, the popular festival is a week-long food and beverage extravaganza. From cooking classes to whiskey tastings and all things 'cue to swanky speakeasies, there is a smorgasbord of options, with local and guest chefs, winemakers, authors, and more. Signature events include the River Street Stroll, featuring a half mile of curated libations along the riverfront, the Grand Reserve Tasting for the true wine connoisseur, the James Beard Celebrity Chef Tour, and the massive Taste of Savannah in the historic Georgia State Railroad Museum. Special packages (including multiple event tickets, accommodations, and more) can be a bargain.

912-232-1223
savannahfoodandwinefest.com

TIP
Sunday's Jazz & Bubbles Brunch is a local favorite.

OTHER GREAT WAYS TO TAKE A BITE (OR GULP) OUT OF SAVANNAH:

Savannah Restaurant Week
Two annually, starting in late January and July
savannahnow.com

Savannah Craft Brew Fest
912-644-6401, savannahcraftbrewfest.com

Savannah Craft Beer Week
781-763-7465, savcraftbeer.com

Savannah Greek Festival
912-236-8256, savannahgreekfest.com

Shalom Y'all Jewish Food Festival
912-233-1547, mickveisrael.org/food-festival

Tybee Wine Festival
912-472-4790, tybeeposttheater.org

EAT (AND DRINK) UP SAVANNAH
ON A CULINARY TOUR

Savannah's culinary scene is easily explored through one or more varied culinary tours with knowledgeable guides, featuring a growing list of tours that draws lots of hungry repeat visitors. The tasty options include: Savannah Taste Experience (First Squares Food Tour and Famous & Secret East Side Food Tour), Southern Flavors Savannah (Taste Tour, Haunted Pub Crawl, and Dessert Tour), Sip n' Shop Savannah Tours (wine, souvenir tumbler, hors d'oeuvres, snacks, and shopping), Savannah Tours & Tales (coffee, chocolate, drinks, and a show), Savannah Walks (haunted pubs and taverns), Full Moon Tours (several beverage-focused tours), Bonnie Blue Tours (Lightly Sauced, Raise a Glass to History), Savannah Pub Tours (Haunted Savannah Pub Crawl), Spooky Savannah Ghost Tours (Haunted Pub Crawl & Ghost Tour), and Damsels & Divas (Haunted Pub Crawl).

> **TIP**
> Don't eat or drink much before one of these tasty tours in Savannah, where they're as hospitable with samples as they are with smiles.

Savannah Taste Experience
912-221-4439
savannahtaste
experience.com

Southern Flavors Savannah
912-695-0577
southernflavors
savannah.com

Savannah Tours & Tales
912-483-2109
savannahtours
andtales.com

Sip n' Shop Savannah Tours
912-373-5501
sipnshopsavannah
tours.com

Savannah Walks
912-385-0577
savannahwalks.com

Full Moon Tours
515-992-0519
(text only)
fullmoontours.com

Bonnie Blue Tours
912-398-2640
bonniebluetours.com

Savannah Pub Tours
912-445-5027
savannahpubtours.
com

Spooky Savannah Ghost Tours
912-667-3156
spookysavannah
ghosttours.com

Damsels & Divas
912-433-4077
damsels-divas-
theodora-ash-tours.
business.site

TOAST AND THANK SERVICE MEMBERS
AT SERVICE BREWING

A veteran-owned and -operated brewery in historic downtown Savannah, Service Brewing donates a portion of every pint sold to veteran-focused charities, making it easy to toast and thank service members of all types. Since 2014, visitors have been enjoying cold beers with military-themed names like Ground Pounder, Rally Point, Compass Rose, and Battlewagon. There are typically twelve beers on tap that offer a selection of beer styles, rotating seasonals, and small-batch brews in a spacious tap room. Quaffers can play darts or ping-pong or just take in the unique design of this welcoming space. All visitors should be sure to interact with the "How Do You Serve?" wall and share how they have served their community and country.

574 Indian St.
912-358-1002, servicebrewing.com

EXTRA CREDIT

Kevin Barry's Irish Pub (117 W River St.) is an extremely popular riverfront destination with great food and live music; but many visitors don't know about their "Hall of Heroes," which is a military and first responders service museum composed of pieces given to pub owner Vic Power, featuring portraits of men and women who gave their lives serving our country.
kevinbarrys.com

SEVERAL OTHER CREATIVE CRAFT BREWERIES IN THE AREA SERVE UNIQUE BEERS AND MUCH MORE (FROM FOOD TO FUN GAMES AND EVENTS).

Coastal Empire Beer Co.
79 Rose Rd.
912-335-2804, coastalempirebeer.com

Moon River Brewing Co.
21 W Bay St.
912-447-0943, moonriverbrewing.com

Southbound Brewing Company
107 E Lathrop Ave.
912-335-1737, southboundbrewing.com

Two Tides Brewing Company
12 W 41st St.
912-667-0706, twotidesbrewing.com

GET THEE
TO THE GREY

The Grey's refurbished 1938 art deco Greyhound bus terminal setting—diner car included—and their vintage take on updated "Southern eats" give a whole new meaning to retro. Opened in 2014, chef/partner and James Beard "Best Chef Southeast" award winner Mashama Bailey and hospitable front-of-the-house founding partner Johno Morisano bring local fare and friendly flair to Savannah's burgeoning dining scene. Southern twists abound, including Bailey's don't-miss charred okra and reimagined "thrills" to end the night. The Grey is more popular than ever after Bailey's Beard win, so making reservations well in advance is highly recommended.

109 Martin Luther King Jr. Blvd.
912-662-5999, thegreyrestaurant.com

EXTRA CREDIT
Situated just blocks away at 109 Jefferson St., The Grey Market is a great New York bodega-like place to head for their Market Burger and a taste of The Grey, with baked goods and larger plates like the fried fish and grits.
thegreymkt.com

BECOME A PART
OF THE BITTY & BEAU'S STORY

The Bitty & Beau's Coffee story is about people as much as it is about coffee (though the coffee and other offerings are great!). It's about people, because the shops are run by people with intellectual and developmental disabilities who greet and serve customers with friendly pride. Founded in 2016 by Amy Wright (2017 CNN Hero of the Year) in Wilmington, North Carolina, Bitty & Beau's Coffee now also has locations in Savannah, Charleston, and Annapolis. The bustling Savannah shop features beloved service, a variety of coffee drinks, sweets, and some great gift options, including Bitty & Beau's items. But you don't have to buy a thing to become part of the Bitty & Beau's story (though you'll want to). Just walk in the door and watch the story unfold.

319 W Congress St.
912-358-7180, bittyandbeauscoffee.com

SAY "OUI"
TO SAVANNAH'S
SAVORY FRENCH CONNECTIONS

Many say Savannah has a European flavor, and that's certainly true when it comes to the city's savory French connections. Magnifique options include: 39 Rue de Jean (brasserie cuisine in an oh-so-French café and bar setting), Circa 1875 French Bistro (locals know to hit the adjacent Gastro Pub when they can't get a table at Circa 1875 "proper"), Café M (French pastries, macarons, quiches, salads, and sandwiches), Le Café Gourmet (house made artisan breads, croissants, crepes, quiches, and soups), and Le Macaron French Pastries (so much more than their colorful macarons).

39 Rue de Jean
605 W Oglethorpe Ave.
912-721-0595
holycityhospitality.com

Circa 1875 French Bistro
48 Whitaker St.
912-443-1875, circa1875.com

Café M
128 E Bay St.
912-712-3342, cafemsavannah.com

Le Café Gourmet
53 Montgomery St.
912-200-3258, lecafegourmet.com

Le Macaron French Pastries
204 W Broughton St.
912-712-5094, lemacaron-us.com

EAT WITH WILD ABANDON
AT THE WYLD

Overlooking a bucolic tidal creek less than 20 minutes from downtown, The Wyld is a world away—and worth the drive. The waterside dock bar and restaurant offers stunning views of the marshland, bocce, a fire pit, and seafood-focused monthly menus. Veteran visitors know to look for starters like seasonal oysters, crab cakes with bitter greens and remoulade, or the scallop corn fritters with habanero honey butter. Keep the seafood theme going with the catch of the day, local shrimp, or the popular fish tacos with locally caught fish steamed in a banana leaf and seasonal Southern-leaning sides with twists.

2740 Livingston Ave.
912-692-1219, thewylddockbar.com

LEARN AND EAT
AT 700 KITCHEN COOKING SCHOOL
AT MANSION ON FORSYTH PARK

Part of the luxurious Mansion on Forsyth Park's many offerings, 700 Kitchen Cooking School has become a popular, tasty, and tasteful Savannah offering. The three-hour classes in the state-of-the-art kitchen classroom are both hands-on and demonstration-only, with light nibbles (think cheese and charcuterie) served during each class and a full meal at the conclusion of the class. With a maximum of sixteen participants, the widely varied classes include hors d'oeuvres, low-country staples, a farmer's market tour (Saturday mornings), ladies night, plant-based cuisine, Taste of 700 Drayton, ethnic classes (from the Caribbean to Europe, Iran, and beyond), and a private dinner with the chef (maximum of eight guests). Cocktails, wine, and beer are available for purchase throughout demonstration-only classes and after the participatory part of the hands-on class.

700 Drayton St.
912-721-5006, mansion.classesbykessler.com

EXTRA CREDIT
Chef Darin Sehnert was hired to develop 700 Kitchen Cooking School and now owns and operates Chef Darin's Kitchen Table in the Starland District at 2514 Abercorn St., Ste 140, which features varied hands-on cooking classes and a great kitchen store.
chefdarin.com

TAKE TEA
(AND MUCH MORE)
AT GRYPHON

Located on Madison Square in the architecturally rich 1926 Scottish Rite Masonic Temple, which served as Solomon's Drugstore for more than seventy years, Gryphon harkens back to another era with white tablecloths, carved mahogany bookcases, and original mortar and pestle stained-glass panels. Now the premier café of the Savannah College of Art and Design (SCAD), traditional afternoon tea is served every day for a true Savannah respite. Featuring a pot of tea—they offer ten varieties daily plus a flavor of the day—along with a selection of tea sandwiches, scones with house-made Devonshire cream and strawberry jam, fresh fruit, and an assortment of freshly made tea sweets, it is a fitting taste of Southern hospitality. Gryphon isn't known just for their traditional teas. It's also popular for lunch, Sunday brunch, and its delectable desserts.

337 Bull St.
912-525-5280, scadgryphon.com

ENJOY AN EVENING WITH A GRANDE DAME
AT ELIZABETH ON 37TH

For fine dining, Savannah's Grande Dame since the early 1980s has been Elizabeth on 37th. Set in a turn-of-the-century Georgian mansion filled with fireplaces, high ceilings, stunning stained glass, and original paintings and ceramics, guests are treated to Savannah culinary traditions with a contemporary flavor. Fans of Elizabeth on 37th know to start with a fresh mozzarella and local tomato salad with herb pecan pesto, balsamic, and truffle oil or local blue crab cake when either is on the menu. Entrée choices like the double-cut Berkshire pork chop with five cheese macaroni and apple-cabbage slaw ooze decadence, and the potato-encrusted American red snapper with brussels sprout hash shows off the bounty of the region like the Grande Dame has done for almost four decades.

105 E 37th St.
912-236-5547, elizabethon37th.net

EXTRA CREDIT
Fine Italian dining is just down the block at La Scala Ristorante (119 E 37th St.).
lascalasavannah.com

14

EAT YOUR FILL IN AN OLD NEIGHBORHOOD FILLING STATION
AT ATLANTIC

Once a neighborhood filling station from the 1930s to the 1960s, Atlantic is now a neighborhood eatery in Savannah's bustling Starland District that conjures up a sense of sharing and camaraderie. Whether you're ordering from it in the sleek dining room, the community table at the bar, or the front or back patios, the menu is filled with tasty small plates—along with a few full entrées—that are perfect for sharing (as is a bottle of wine from one of Savannah's best wine lists). Depending on what's on the menu, begin with the beet carpaccio sprinkled with pistachios, fried capers, and a champagne vinaigrette. Share the roasted shishito peppers in a butternut squash coulis. And revel in the ratatouille. But no matter what you do, if it's on the menu, don't miss the seared pork belly with a corn, field peas, and miso compound butter succotash. Trust us.

102 E Victory Dr.
912-417-8887, atlanticsavannah.com

EAT WHERE THE ELITE EAT IN THEIR BARE FEET
AT THE ORIGINAL CRAB SHACK

The Original Crab Shack on Tybee Island is where "the elite eat in their bare feet." With waterfront dining on Chimney Creek inside and out, plus three full-service bars, The Original Crab Shack is known for raw, steamed, boiled, and low-country–style seafood, as well as ribs, barbecue, chicken, and more. They are also famous for their fun drinks in souvenir cups and a unique interactive "Gator Lagoon" with more than seventy-five alligators (they sell bags of gator food). To keep it casual, they don't take reservations—and they do let guests dining outside on the deck take off their shoes!

40 Estill Hammock Rd., Tybee Island
912-414-4122, thecrabshack.com

EXTRA CREDIT
For a taste of the low country when not in Savannah, visit
The Original Crab Shack's mail-order website to order a "A Taste of
the LOCOuntry TO GO" (including free shipping).
locotogo.net

GET LUCKY
AT LEOPOLD'S ICE CREAM

With lines occasionally down the block, people flock to this throwback ice cream parlor that celebrated its 100th anniversary in 2019. Founded by three brothers from Greece and now run by descendants of that original family, the legendary handcrafted ice cream is served in two dozen classic flavors (including the original 1919 Tutti Frutti—rum ice cream with candied fruit and fresh roasted Georgia pecans), rotating seasonal flavors (like Japanese Cherry Blossom and Pumpkin Spice), decadent banana splits, overstuffed sundaes, ice cream sandwiches on scratch-made cookies, milkshakes, ice cream sodas, floats, and specialty hot beverages. Most of their ice cream ingredients and toppings are prepared in-house, as are their sandwiches and signature salads.

212 E Broughton St.
912-234-4442, leopoldsicecream.com

TIP
Anytime is a lucky time to head to Leopold's, but the wait is typically the shortest right when they open at 11 a.m. or late in the evening.

CHOW DOWN ON A BURGER AND BEER
AT CRYSTAL BEER PARLOR

One of Savannah's oldest restaurants in what was once the Gerken Family Grocery Store, "The Crystal" opened in 1933 and is reported to be one of the first restaurants to serve alcohol after the repeal of Prohibition. Enjoy more than eighty-five beers—including a selection of "Beers of Our Fathers" (hard-to-find, time-honored beers) and a host of burgers, including an Au Poivre burger, Greek lamb burger, meatloaf burger, bison burger, the N.O.G.S. (North of Gaston Street) burger with bacon, balsamic marinated sautéed portobello mushrooms, Brie cheese, and fresh spinach, or try the classic griddled half-pound Crystal Burger, which has been on the menu for more than eighty years. Splurge on the onion rings, which are always freshly prepared and fried to order.

301 W Jones St.
912-349-1000, crystalbeerparlor.com

DO DATE NIGHT RIGHT
AT 700 DRAYTON

What better way to celebrate date night than with a romantic table for two at 700 Drayton in The Kessler Collection's Mansion on Forsyth Park. The stunning ambiance is filled with world-class artwork, fireplaces, and original wood flooring and trim in a historic 1888 mansion overlooking the park. Evening fare focuses on simply prepared regional specialties, fish, and chophouse steaks. If it's on the menu, enjoy the tête-à-tête with several shareable plates, such as the Hunter's Board with soppressata, truffle chicken mousse, speck, goat and cambozola cheese, and lingonberry jam or the Southbound Lager beer mussels, dressed in butter, Fresno peppers, onions, and fennel and served with a warm baguette. Of course, spending the night at Mansion on Forsyth Park provides the perfect way to complete a date night done right.

700 Drayton St.
912-721-5002, kesslercollection.com/700-drayton

EXTRA CREDIT
Mansion on Forsyth owner Richard C. Kessler is a renowned art collector, and a pre- or post-dinner tour of the art collection in the adjacent hotel is highly recommended.

GET IN THE SPIRIT
AT GHOST COAST DISTILLERY

Downtown's Ghost Coast Distillery, which is just down the street from Service Brewing Co., is a great place to head when you want to get a little spirited. They offer a wide range of spirits that are available at the distillery and on bar shelves around town and beyond, including straight bourbon whiskey, honey flavored whiskey, ginger-flavored whiskey, vodka, orange-flavored vodka, tiki spiced rum, Burl Gin, Chalmers Maraschino (cherry almond liqueur), Carthusian bitters, Fernet bitters, and Georgia Peach Liqueur. Spirits carried at the distillery include rum, whiskey, elder flower, sweet aperitif, Tommy agave, curacao, and Italian bitters. Creative cocktails are extremely popular at Ghost Coast Distillery, as are their fun tours.

641 Indian St.
912-298-0071, ghostcoastdistillery.com

SATISFY YOUR SWEET TOOTH
AT SAVANNAH'S CANDY KITCHEN

Specializing in "Southern candy," including pralines, gophers, caramels, chocolates, fudge, popcorn, nuts, log rolls, toffee, brittle, and so much more (including many gluten-free options and gift packages), Savannah's Kitchen is the perfect place for a unique Savannah souvenir. Along with their two downtown locations, Savannah's Candy Kitchen can also be found in Charleston, Hartsfield-Jackson Atlanta International Airport (two locations), Nashville, and Oxon Hill, Maryland (National Harbor). They also offer mail-order.

225 E River St., 912-233-8411
318 West St. Julian St., 912-201-9501
savannahcandy.com

EXTRA CREDIT

Situated just down the street from the Savannah's Candy Kitchen River Street location, The Peanut Shop of Savannah (407 E River St.) features hand-roasted "Gold Standard" peanuts, seasoned peanuts, chocolates, and brittles, plus other foods and Southern-leaning gifts.
thepeanutshop.com

QUAFF A QUEEN OF SIAM COCKTAIL
AT PROHIBITION

You don't need a secret password or knock on the door to enjoy a cocktail and more at downtown's Prohibition. Of course, this classic speakeasy in a classy 1920s setting features iconic and contemporary cocktails, but those in the know also stay for creative cuisine. Their signature Queen of Siam cocktail tops the list literally and figuratively, thanks to a perfect mix of G4 Blanco Tequila, house-made Thai chili pineapple syrup, grapefruit shrub, and lime. The brunch, dinner, and late-night menus mean that you won't leave hungry, with Prohibition's delectable hamburger remaining a favorite to order since opening. Veterans of Prohibition also rave about the daily happy hour, where bargain-priced drinks and snacks await. There's a similar Prohibition experience awaiting in Charleston.

125 Martin Luther King Jr. Blvd.
912-200-9255, prohibitionsavannah.com

SAY "CHEERS"
TO THE AMERICAN PROHIBITION MUSEUM

Located along Savannah's City Market, the American Prohibition Museum is most definitely not your typical "dry" museum. The highly professional exhibits dramatically portray the Prohibition movement, era, and repeal, from the mid-1800s to 1933, including such intoxicating exhibits as Temperance Movement, Carry Nation, Rum Runner, Moonshine, Flapper Craze, Crime & Gangsters, the Origins of NASCAR, and Happy Days (repeal in 1933). There's even an operating speakeasy toward the end of the self-guided tour, with craft cocktails, wines, and beers that trace their roots back to Prohibition. They even offer cocktail classes to learn the history and secrets of classic cocktails.

209 W St. Julian St.
912-344-9243, americanprohibitionmuseum.com

EAT LOCAL
AT HUSK

With ever-popular sister outposts in Charleston, Greenville, and Nashville, Husk Savannah pays homage to the indigenous ingredients and heirloom products of coastal Georgia. Located in the heart of the historic district, the Southern-inspired menu highlights local and regional ingredients and farmers and changes daily according to seasonality and availability. Dishes on the changing menu include country ham biscuits with purple ribbon cane syrup from Sapelo Island, sassafras glazed pork ribs with pickled Georgia peaches and butter beans, or Georgia shrimp and grits with tomato and sweet corn, celebrating the regional bounty while striving to refine Savannah cooking and change the way we look at Southern cuisine. There's no dining experience quite like that found at Husk.

12 W Oglethorpe Ave.
912-349-2600, husksavannah.com

SQUIRREL AWAY SOME PIZZA
AT SQUIRREL'S

Located in Savannah's Starland District, Squirrel's owner and chef Chris Dickerson (also of Jacksonville's popular Corner Taco) is guided by the spirit of Italian pizza craft techniques, including both Neapolitan and Roman styles, with a focus on ingredient-rich pizzas of crisp, airy crust, and all-American ingredients. Dickerson uses live fire (built from pecan wood) in a Prevasi oven to craft his pizzas and other craveable dishes. Along with his creative red and white pizzas, there are salads, sandwiches, shareable bites, and well-curated wine, beer, and cocktail lists.

2218 Bull St.
912-335-7873, squirrelspizza.com

GRAB A SANDWICH
AT ZUNZI'S

Locals and visitors alike rave about the sandwiches at Zunzi's for good reason. Zunzi's is a South African–inspired takeout, delivery, and catering restaurant in the heart of downtown. The eclectic menu is influenced by the South African, Italian, Swiss, and Dutch heritage of Zunzi's founders, John and Gabriella Debeer. The sandwiches certainly take star billing, including perennial favorite Boerewors on a Roll (French bread, South African sausage, grilled peppers and onions, brown gravy, and dank sauce, a spicy, diced tomato–based all-purpose sauce), but the various build-your-own bowls and plates, sides, sauces, and more make a Zunzi's order challenging. They also have an outpost in Atlanta.

108 E York St.
912-443-9555, zunzis.com

TIP
Zunzi's offers a happy hour from 4 to 7 p.m. daily, with half-off beer and wine, providing the perfect pairing for a Zunzi's sandwich and more.

ENJOY A TASTE OF SAVANNAH
WITH PAULA DEEN

Paula Deen's landmark restaurant The Lady & Sons has been a Savannah tradition since 1989. Whether it's the famed fried chicken and much more from the overflowing buffet or the tasty fried green tomatoes, crab stew, shrimp and grits, and more from the à la carte menu, there's a reason The Lady & Sons stays packed for lunch and supper. The sprawling shop adjacent to the restaurant also stays busy, thanks to Deen's cookbooks, cookware, home goods, food items, and more. For a different Deen dining experience just eight miles east of downtown on Turner Creek, Paula Deen's Creek House features Southern classics and seafood favorites in a coastal Savannah setting. She owns and operates it with her sons, Jamie and Bobby—both famed television personalities and cookbook authors in their own right.

The Lady & Sons
102 W Congress St.
912-233-2600

Paula Deen's Creek House
104 Bryan Woods Rd.
912-344-4634, pauladeen.com

EXTRA CREDIT
Paula Deen has a third restaurant concept called Paula Deen's Family Kitchen, with locations in Myrtle Beach, South Carolina, Foley, Alabama, Pigeon Forge, Tennessee—and counting.

SIP SAVANNAH
AT THE GEORGIA TASTING ROOM

Conveniently situated in the heart of City Market, The Georgia Tasting Room is an efficient and fun way to get a big taste of Savannah and the rest of the Peach State. The tasty concept and experience are simple. They stock craft beers from Savannah and surrounding Georgia areas and regional wines and goods for tasting and purchase. Wine smoothies are a specific specialty at The Georgia Tasting Room, with lots of varied flavors and bargain-priced tastes and purchase possibilities. The Peach Sangria Wine Smoothie is particularly popular.

306 W Julian St.
912-495-5118, thegeorgiatastingroom.com

GET FOXY
AT FOXY LOXY CAFÉ AND BEYOND

Local entrepreneur Jen Jenkins loves keeping locals and visitors caffeinated and well fed at her varied hotspots. The "Foxy" flagship location is Foxy Loxy Café, in the heart of Midtown, which is a café, bakery, Tex-Mex cantina, and popular live music and events venue (with a great courtyard where Jenkins loves hanging out). Back in downtown proper, The Coffee Fox features pour-over coffees from popular Savannah-based PERC Coffee Roaster, tasty pastries, cheese boards, beer, and more (there's also another Coffee Fox hotpsot in Savannah's west end on Louisville Rd.). Just off Troup Square, Fox & Fig Café is a plant-based vegan café with an eclectic brunch-centric menu that's served all day, as well as house-made cashew hemp lattes and other coffee drinks featuring nondairy milks, Leopold's coconut cream milkshakes, wine, beer, and more.

Foxy Loxy Café	**Fox & Fig Café**
1919 Bull St.	321 Habersham St.
912-401-0543, foxyloxycafe.com	912-297-6759, foxandfigcafe.com

The Coffee Fox
102 W Broughton St., 912-401-0399
1103 Louisville Rd., 912-525-2336
thecoffeefox.com

EXTRA CREDIT
Jen Jenkins also co-owns and operates Henny Penny Art Space & Café (1514 Bull St.) with the folks from Scribble Art Studio, with craft coffees, fresh pastries, and space for creating arts and crafts. hennypennycafe.com

EAT FAMILY-STYLE
AT MRS. WILKES DINING ROOM

Lunch in Mrs. Wilkes Dining Room is like a typical family meal in households across the South. Community tables of ten are filled with family, friends, and strangers and close to two dozen shareable platters and bowls filled with rotating Southern staples like fried chicken (sinful and, thankfully, available every day), beef stew, meat loaf, cornbread dressing, candied yams, black-eyed peas, okra and tomatoes, butter beans, mashed potatoes, pickled beets, collard greens, and more. To make it feel even more like home, it's first come, first served. Lunch is served Monday to Friday 11 a.m. to 2 p.m. sharp; you clear your own dishes and they accept only cash or check. You might even be inspired to kiss Mrs. Wilkes's granddaughter, the current proprietress, on your way out.

107 W Jones St.
912-232-5997, mrswilkes.com

EXTRA CREDIT
To complete the Wilkes "family" experience, book a stay at the Wilkes Pied-a-Terre, a Southern-style apartment above the restaurant. A stay includes two gift cards for lunch.

SAVOR SOMETHING BAKED WITH LOVE
AT BACK IN THE DAY BAKERY

Whether it's the sweet smells of freshly baked confections or the warm ambiance of the whitewashed walls and retro décor (think vintage mixers, flour canisters, and antique pendant chandeliers), you'll feel like you are back in the days of your childhood at the Starland District's Back in the Day Bakery. A magical display case bursts with rainbow colors of cupcakes, pies, cookies, bars, and brownies. Those in the know come for the savory side as well. Morning people flock to the tarts, quiches, and the Sunny Day Biscuit with egg frittata, bacon, and house-made seasonal jam. The flaky layers in their all-butter buttermilk biscuits make it their number one seller. And the breads—don't even get us started on the piquant breads and creative sandwich fillings.

2403 Bull St.
912-495-9292, backinthedaybakery.com

DINE AT
A SAVANNAH CLASSIC
AT THE OLDE PINK HOUSE

Legend has it that the cotton candy pink exterior of the aptly named Olde Pink House resulted from the deep red of the original bricks bleeding through the white stucco of this 1771 Georgian mansion. Truth or fiction—what we do know is that the Southern menu bleeds through this romantic dining experience. Dining options include the ornate dining rooms throughout the house, which are filled with heart pine planks, crystal chandeliers, fireplaces, and the more intimate and casual tavern downstairs. The oh-so-Savannah gussied up sautéed local shrimp with country ham gravy and cheddar cheese grit cakes, fall-off-the-bone braised pork shank with macaroni and cheese and collards, and collards, the iconic crispy scored flounder, and much more will make you think you've died and gone to Southern heaven.

23 Abercorn St.
912-232-4286, theoldepinkhouserestaurant.com

TIP
Reservations are highly recommended.

DINE DELECTABLY WITH A VIEW
AT THE DECK BEACHBAR AND KITCHEN

Oceanfront dining is less than twenty miles away on Savannah's Tybee Island and The Deck—nestled within the dunes—offers up killer views and a classic beachfront vibe. It's all about the seafood here, with dining inside (plenty of windows bring in the ocean breeze) or out on the deck. Start with the crab cakes, served up with charred pineapple chutney and arugula. Favorite entreés include Buffalo shrimp tacos with cilantro slaw and blue cheese crema and the massive seafood platter. Serving two to three people with beer-battered tempura cod, grilled shrimp, fried calamari, snow crab legs, ahi tuna poke, corn on the cob, malt vinegar fries, sweet potato fries, and island slaw, you'd better come hungry.

404 Butler Ave., Tybee Island
912-786-4745, thedecktybee.com

EXTRA CREDIT
The Deck's friendly Aussie owner, Anthony Debreceny, also owns three other Savannah favorites (and counting): The Collins Quarter (151 Bull St.,), which is famed for its Aussie-style brunch; The Collins Quarter on Forsyth (a sister restaurant and more in Forsyth Park); and The Fitzroy (9 Drayton St.), which is an Aussie-inspired gastro pub.
thecollinsquarter.com, thefitzroysavannah.com

FIND YOUR SWEET SPOT
AT LULU'S CHOCOLATE BAR

Devoted to scratch-made desserts and creative cocktails, Lulu's Chocolate Bar is definitely on the "Why didn't I think of that?" list. Start at the bar (daily happy hour until 7:00 p.m.) and enjoy one of their twenty different martinis—many of which feature chocolate, like the Lulutini or the Milky Way—or a chocolate beer or deep ruby red wine. Then move on to dessert with a slice of Lulu's strawberry suspension cake, white chocolate chip cheesecake, triple chocolate mousse on a disc of pure chocolate and a chocolate sauce bath, the "Big Cookie"—a giant delicious mini-dark-chocolate chip cookie cut into a pie wedge, heated, and served with vanilla ice cream—or a sultry cheese board.

42 Martin Luther King Jr. Blvd.
912-480-4564, luluschocolatebar.com

EXTRA CREDIT
Chocoholics will also love learning about Chocolat by Adam Turoni (323 W Broughton St. and 236 Bull St.), featuring locally handcrafted chocolates and more from a Culinary Institute of America graduate.
chocolat.com

MAKE A BEELINE
TO B'S CRACKLIN' BBQ

Ask anyone in town where to get some classic Southern barbecue, and most folks will point you in the direction of B's Cracklin' BBQ. Bryan Furman (along with his wife, Nikki) are smokin' up whole heritage-breed hogs that they raise themselves and putting out plates of pulled pork, brisket, ribs, and chicken that have folks calling him Georgia's new king of barbeque. With a unique sauce that's part Carolina tangy mustard and part sweet Georgia peaches, Furman cooks everything the old-fashioned way—low and slow over wood. Add in sides that he learned from his momma, like macaroni and cheese, collard greens, barbecue beans, and hash and rice, and you've got the South in your mouth.

12409 White Bluff Rd.
912-330-6921, bscracklinbbq.com

GET SOULFUL
AT NAROBIA'S GRITS AND GRAVY

A true Savannahian take on soul food, Narobia's takes grits and gravy to another level. Heaping servings of grits come with varied gravy combinations, including shrimp, sausage (beef or turkey), lamb with green peppers, onions and mushrooms, or the tasty crab stew loaded with succulent shrimp, crab meat, green peppers, onions, and just the perfect amount of spice. Or simply get the brown gravy with liver and onions, fried flounder, salmon patty, or a ribeye on top. All breakfast plates come with two eggs any way you'd like them and toast or a butter-kissed biscuit. If grits aren't your thing, try the sausage gravy over biscuits. Or substitute the grits for hash browns or French fries.

2019 Habersham St.
912-231-0563, narobiasgrits.restaurantwebexpert.com

EXTRA CREDIT
Downtown's downstairs Alligator Soul is a great place to head for farm-to-table seasonal New Orleans–style soul food and more.
alligatorsoul.com

EAT, DRINK, AND BE VERY MERRY
AT PLANT RIVERSIDE

When it opened in late 2019, Plant Riverside District immediately became another Savannah success story that made it easy to eat, drink, and be very merry right on (and above) the Savannah River. The 4.5-acre, $330 million-plus project at the site of the former historic Georgia Power Plant has brought new life to the western end of downtown Savannah, thanks to three boutique hotels, more than a dozen different dining options, three rooftop bars, lots of shops, an art gallery, an outdoor park honoring Martin Luther King Jr., an outdoor entertainment space, an indoor live concert venue, and more. Quite simply, Plant Riverside delivered what only visionary Richard C. Kessler, owner of The Kessler Collection, could—yet another great place to eat, drink, and be very merry in Savannah.

plantriverside.com

EAT BREAKFAST ALL DAY
AT CLARY'S CAFÉ

What's better than a classic diner-style breakfast? A classic diner-style breakfast joint that serves breakfast all day. Clary's Cafe has been serving it up all day every day since 1903, and locals swear by it. Naturally, they have eggs in all styles and lots of omelettes, all served with buttered grits or breakfast potatoes and toast or biscuits. But then there are eggs Benedict (try the crab cake Benedict), French toast (get it stuffed with strawberries and cream), and Georgia pecan pancakes. And don't miss the specials, like their famous, freshly made corned beef hash (they make their own whole corned beef briskets in the back) or the Hoppel Poppel (scrambled eggs with salami, potatoes, onion, and green pepper).

404 Abercorn St.
912-233-0402, claryscafe.com

AMONG LOTS OF OPTIONS ACROSS TOWN, THERE ARE MANY OTHER UNIQUE SAVANNAH HOTSPOTS FOR BREAKFAST OR BRUNCH.

B. Matthew's Eatery
324 E Bay St.
912-233-1319
bmatthewseatery.com

Café M
128 E Bay St.
912-712-3342
cafemsavannah.com

Goose Feathers Café
39 Barnard St.
912-233-4683
goosefeatherscafe.com

Huey's
115 E River St.
912-234-7385
hueysontheriver.net

J. Christopher's
122 E Liberty St.
912-236-7494
(Plus, more than twenty
other Georgia locations
and two in Tennessee.)
jchristophers.com

Mirabelle
313 Abercorn St.
912-231-3936
mirabellesavannah.com

The Collins Quarter
151 Bull St.
912-777-4147
thecollinsquarter.com

The Funky Brunch Café
304 Broughton St.
912-234-3050
thefunkybrunchcafe.com

The Ordinary Pub
217½ W Broughton St.
912-238-5130
theordinarypub.com

Two Cracked Eggs Café
202 E Bay St.
912-201-1319
twocrackedeggscafe.com

TAKE A BITE OUT OF HISTORY
AT THE PIRATES' HOUSE

Sure, The Pirates' House is touristy, but both locals and visitors flock to it for good reason. Located just seven blocks west from where General Oglethorpe landed in 1733, the building first opened as an inn for seafarers in 1733, quickly becoming a meeting point for sailors—and pirates. Today, this historic house offers a peek into Savannah's pirating past while serving tasty food and beverages. The menus lean toward Southern fare and seafood, including popular "Captain Flint's Favorites," such as shrimp and grits and crab cakes. There's also a great kids' menu and adult beverages, including Chatham Artillery Punch (a traditional Savannah cocktail that every bartender in town should be able to explain and prepare), Skull Crusher, Pirates' Pleasure, Bloody Pirate, Dark & Stormy, Savannah Tea, and rum tasting flights. Be sure to check out the treasures in their gift shop.

20 E Broad St.
912-233-5757, thepirateshouse.com

TIP

Savannah is one of few cities with an "open container" policy, with city laws allowing possession and consumption of one alcoholic beverage in an open container (sixteen ounces maximum) on the streets within downtown's historic district borders (generally north of Jones Street).

Lucas Theatre for the Arts
Photo courtesy of SCAD

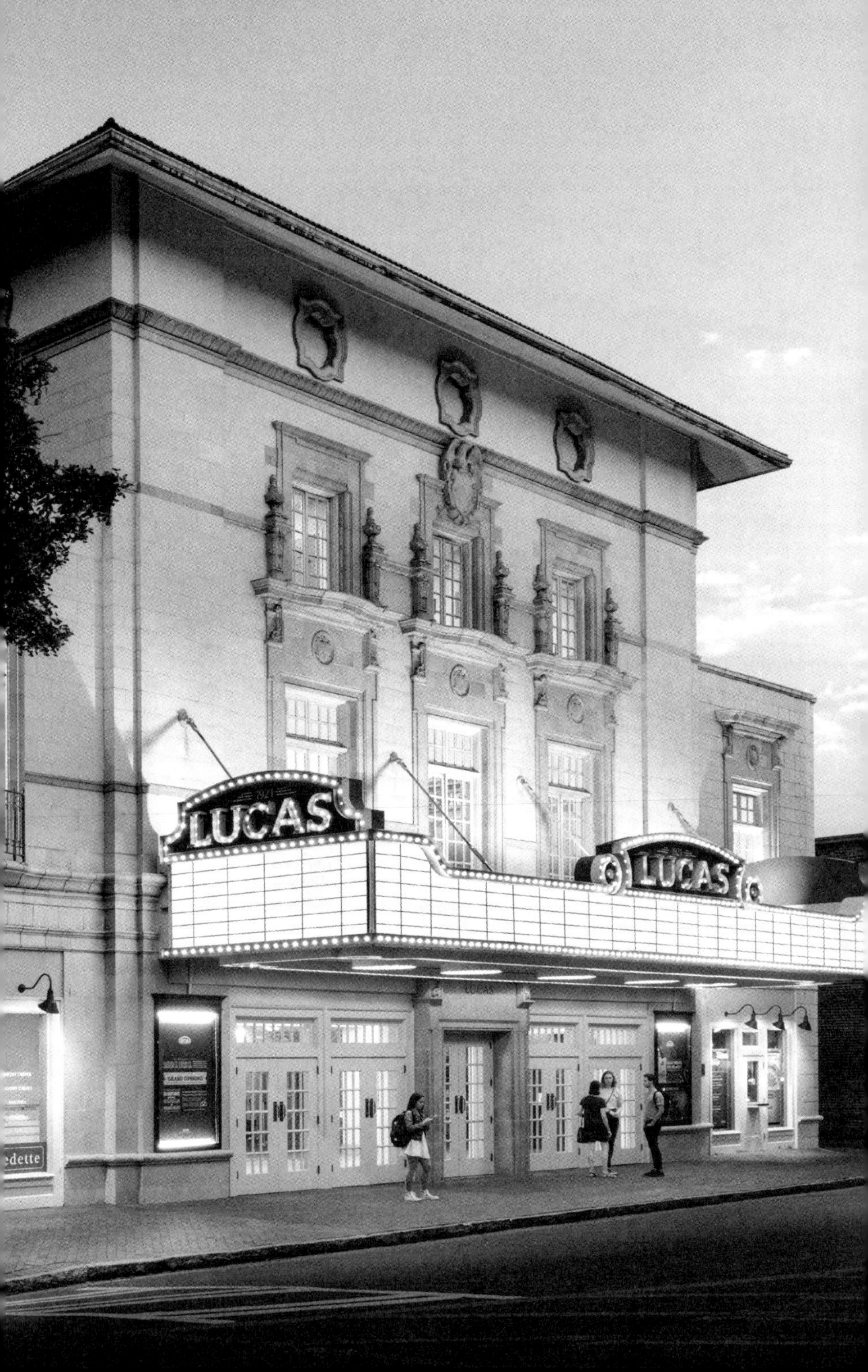

MUSIC AND ENTERTAINMENT

TUNE INTO
THE SAVANNAH MUSIC FESTIVAL

The Savannah Music Festival has become one of the world's top cross-genre music festivals, drawing artists and attendees from around the globe with a wide array of performances in a variety of venues throughout the city. Taking place over fifteen days during Savannah's peak azalea season from late March to early April, the Savannah Music Festival features jazz, country, folk, classical, chamber music, and so much more. Even veteran festival attendees might not know that the Savannah Music Festival actually operates year-round to produce a music education curriculum and semester-end concerts ("Musical Explorers"), an annual high school jazz competition ("Swing Central Jazz"), a workshop and mentorship program for young acoustic musicians ("Acoustic Music Seminar"), and a weekly radio series ("Savannah Music Festival LIVE").

912-525-5050
savannahmusicfestival.org

CATCH A SHOW
AT THE HISTORIC SAVANNAH THEATRE

Situated just off Chippewa Square on bustling Bull Street, The Historic Savannah Theatre originally opened its doors back in 1818 and has welcomed the likes of Lillian Russell, Oscar Wilde, W. C. Fields, and even baseball great Ty Cobb, who appeared in "The College Widow" in 1911. Today, the remodeled (with comfort in mind) historic theatre features live performances, short and long runs of varied shows, and ongoing "house" shows like "Savannah Live" and "A Christmas Tradition." With eight singers and a live band, "Savannah Live" features two hours of high-energy Motown, Broadway, pop, rock and roll, and more. No matter what's on the schedule, The Historic Savannah Theatre is well worth a visit.

222 Bull St.
912-233-7764, savannahtheatre.com

GET YOUR GAME AND GRUB ON
AT THE CHROMATIC DRAGON

The Chromatic Dragon is a gamer's paradise that seemingly has it all, including console games like Mortal Kombat and Mario Kart to board games like Ticket to Ride and Settlers of Catan, party games (from Taboo to Cards Against Humanity), and even traditional bar games, including cornhole, Jenga, trivia, and more. And the Savannah area is home to two locations (downtown and out in nearby Pooler), making it twice as easy to get your game and grub on with like-minded gamers and those who want to learn the ropes. However, The Chromatic Dragon is also an eater's and drinker's paradise, thanks to a menu of creative pub grub with gamer-oriented names, as well creative elixirs and other beverages that pair well with games of choice.

514 Martin Luther King Jr. Blvd.
912-289-0350

400 Pooler Pkwy., Pooler
912-200-9381

chromaticdragon.com

JAZZ IT UP
AT GOOD TIMES JAZZ BAR & RESTAURANT

Owner Stephen T. Moore's love of good music, wine, and food was the driving force behind opening Savannah hotspot Good Times Jazz Bar & Restaurant. With a full slate of live music nightly and a renowned wine and cocktail list and dining menus, Good Times makes for a good time any day. Serving lunch, dinner, and popular Sunday Gospel Brunch, the creative menu features local seafood, salads, sandwiches, soups, bar food choices, and more. The wine list is widely varied (ask about "preferred" wines), while the cocktail list features several signature drinks, including bourbon-driven Broughton Street Blues and their Good Times Mule. Live music generally runs from 7 to 10 p.m. nightly and for the Gospel Sunday Brunch from 11 a.m. to 3 p.m.

107 W Broughton St.
912-236-2226, goodtimesjazzbar.com

GO GREEN ON ST. PATRICK'S DAY
IN SAVANNAH

Savannah's St. Patrick's Day Parade and Celebration has long been known as one of the top St. Patrick's Day celebrations outside of Ireland, making it easy to go green on St. Patrick's Day in Savannah. The St. Patrick's Day Parade starts on Broughton Street and runs through downtown before ending on Bull Street, with many viewing and seating options available. However, downtown Savannah is one big party before, during, and after the parade (and even the day before), including lots of live music, dance parties, interactive artists, food and beverage areas, and activities along the St. Patrick's Day hubs of River Street and City Market, as well as area Irish-leaning bars (like Kevin Barry's Irish Pub and O'Connell's Irish Pub). Locals also know to head to Forsyth Park's famed fountain about a week before St. Patrick's Day, when the fountain's water mysteriously turns green—possibly the work of leprechauns.

912-233-4804
savannahsaintpatricksday.com

EXTRA CREDIT
The mid-afternoon Tybee Island Irish Heritage Parade on St. Patrick's Day provides a unique "island" option as well. It starts at Tybee City Hall and proceeds down Butler Avenue to Tybrisa Street.
visittybee.com

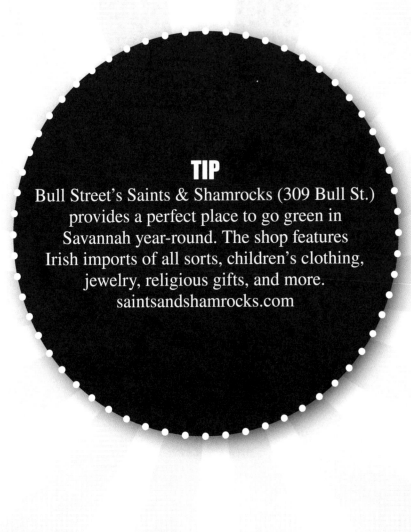

TIP

Bull Street's Saints & Shamrocks (309 Bull St.) provides a perfect place to go green in Savannah year-round. The shop features Irish imports of all sorts, children's clothing, jewelry, religious gifts, and more. saintsandshamrocks.com

CATCH A SHOW
AT TYBEE POST THEATER

Located in the heart of Tybee Island's Fort Screven Historic District, Tybee Post Theater was built back in 1930 as a movie house for soldiers stationed at the Fort Screven military base. It went dark in the mid-1960s, but it was reborn some fifty years later in 2015 as a performing arts and movie venue for Tybee Island residents and visitors. The landmark now features a concert hall for live music, dance, and comedy; a stage for local and touring theater groups; a movie house for first-run, classic, and children's films; a cultural venue for readings, recitals, and educational programs; and a unique venue for weddings, private screenings, photo shoots, and more. Plus, along with popcorn, candy, and other snacks, they serve beer and wine!

10 Van Horne Ave., Tybee Island
912-472-4790, tybeeposttheater.org

JAM
AT THE SAVANNAH JAZZ FESTIVAL

The annual Savannah Jazz Festival has been an iconic week-long event for decades, and it is distinguished by more free performances of world-class jazz and blues than any event in the region. The festival happens each year in late September and attracts more than 40,000 attendees to varied venues across the city and three magical evenings in Forsyth Park. World-renowned performers who have played at the Festival over the years have included Ray Charles, Stanley Turrentine, Ben Tucker, Doreen Kichens, Wycliffe Gordon, Shirley Horne, Eddie Pazant, Joey DeFrancesco, Bernie Williams, Chuck Leavell, and Anat Cohen. With so many free shows (typically more than two dozen) and lots of value-priced options, this fan favorite festival keeps the spirit of jazz doing its important work of uniting all races and classes through one of America's major musical genres.

savannahjazzfest.com

TIP
Varied "VIP Access" options are great for serious jazz fans.

CHANNEL THE SPIRIT OF LADY CHABLIS
AT A CLUB ONE DRAG SHOW

Made famous in the book and movie *Midnight in the Garden of Good and Evil*, drag show queen Lady Chablis sadly passed away in 2016. But her spirit lives on at downtown's bustling three-story Club One. There's a popular drag show on most Thursday, Friday, Saturday, and Sunday nights in Club One's Bay Café. Performers vary, and many have a loyal following, like Lady Chablis. The Bay Café also serves food, including a dozen different "Dawg Pound" hot dogs—like The Threesome (chili, nacho cheese, and onions) and Three Little Pigs (bacon, barbecue pork, American cheese, and Chablis sauce). Other Club One draws include varied happy hours, bingo, karaoke (including a "topless" version), star search nights, and more.

1 Jefferson St.
912-232-0200, clubone-online.com

44

CATCH A FILM (AND MORE) AT HISTORIC LUCAS THEATRE

Originally opened on December 26, 1921 (they showed *Hard Luck* and *Camille*) and completely renovated before reopening in late 2000 to rave reviews, Lucas Theatre for the Arts features varied films, concerts, and other events, including several series throughout the year. It's now operated by the Savannah College of Art and Design (SCAD) and includes Vedette, a SCAD café featuring crepes, pastries, coffees, teas, and more. *Vedette* is the French word for "film star," and the café's name is also a nod to SCAD's campus in Lacoste, France. The Lucas Theatre for the Arts is also the home of the Savannah Film Festival in late October (savannahfilmfestival.com).

32 Abercorn St.
912-525-5051, lucastheatre.org

TIP
The lobby's concession stand is open one hour before showtimes and features happy hour pricing for everyone (not just those with a ticket).

SEE A BIG BAND SHOW
WITH THE
FABULOUS EQUINOX ORCHESTRA

There's nothing quite like the sound of a big band and Savannah's own Fabulous Equinox Orchestra, and their busy schedule around town makes it easy to see a big band show. Founded by Jeremy Davis ("The Kingpin," band leader, tenor sax, and vocals) and Clay Johnson ("Mr. Showtime," the voice, and trombone), The Fabulous Equinox Orchestra typically features about sixteen other members, and they play a bevy of recognizable hits from the big band era and beyond, as well as their own original arrangements. The "Great American Songbook" and beyond (including original arrangements ranging from Ray Charles to Johnny Cash, Texas Swing, '80s pop, disco, and spicy Louisiana music) are performed with style and energy, making every show special.

equinoxorchestra.com

EXTRA CREDIT

Generally, once a month The Fabulous Equinox Orchestra takes to the stage at the Peregrin, situated atop the luxurious Perry Lane Hotel (256 E Perry St.). It's a great venue for them to try out new material. Although while VIP tables sell out quickly, general admission is free and open to the public. Arrive early!
perrylanehotel.com

SPORTS AND RECREATION

CONQUER
THE TALMADGE MEMORIAL BRIDGE

Featuring the iconic Talmadge Bridge over the Savannah River, the Enmarket Savannah Bridge Run in early December has become a fun tradition for both participants and spectators. Bridge Run Day actually consists of a number of different races and a popular post-race party with awards, beer, Brunswick stew, live music, and more. The race options include a 5K (one trip across the bridge), a 10K (two bridge crossings), the Double Pump (runners run both the 5K and the 10K for three bridge crossings), and a Kids Run downtown of about a quarter mile.

savannahbridgerun.com

EXTRA CREDIT

Women looking for a longer run will want
to check out the Savannah Women's Half
& 5K, which includes a popular Fashion Fitness
Expo. In addition, Savannah's Rock 'n' Roll
Marathon in early November is part of a
national series and is an equally popular
race around downtown and beyond.
savannahwomenshalf.com
runrocknroll.com/savannah

CATCH SOME AIR
WITH TYBEE AIRBOATS

Inspired by the popular airboat tours in South Florida, Tybee Airboats brought the concept to the beautiful open water and shallow creeks surrounding Tybee Island. Intimate tours are typically offered daily (depending on the weather) and are part history tour and part nature tour. Two tour options include dolphin and other wildlife sightings on a twenty-five-minute Cockspur Loop with views of historic Fort Pulaski and the Cockspur Island Lighthouse or a one-hour Back River Loop to the nature preserve and wildlife Mecca of Little Tybee Island (which is actually twice the size of Tybee Island). Those who want to extend their stay on the island to enjoy a popular nature walk can hop on the next airboat for the return trip.

3 Old U.S. Highway 80, Tybee Island
912-661-9225, tybeeairboats.com

TAKE A RIVERBOAT CRUISE
ON THE SAVANNAH RIVER

The Savannah River has played a big role in the history and success of the city, and a riverboat cruise is a great way to "see" the city in a different light. Founded by Capt. Jonathan H. Claughton in 1991 and long known for their varied offerings, Savannah Riverboat Cruises features two elegant vessels (the six-hundred-passenger *Savannah River Queen* and the one-thousand-passenger *Georgia Queen*) decked out in red, white, and blue, with two climate-controlled dining decks and an open-air third deck. Tour options include sightseeing cruises, lunch cruises, dinner cruises, brunch cruises, gospel cruises, sunset cruises, moonlight cruises, and special seasonal and holiday offerings. All the tours leave the convenient downtown River Street dock, which is right next to the exact location where General James Oglethorpe first landed in Savannah.

9 E River St.
912-232-6404, savannahriverboat.com

SPEND A NIGHT (OR TWO) ACROSS THE RIVER
WITH WESTIN

Situated just across the Savannah River from downtown, Hutchinson Island and The Westin Savannah Harbor Golf Resort & Spa provide a great haven (and exploration base) for a night (or two), regardless of whether you even head across the river via the frequent and free shuttle. You never really have to leave the 403-room property if you don't want to, in that the full-service resort has practically everything needed for a stay. The possibilities at the Westin include a variety of accommodations options, including many rooms and suites overlooking the river, a multitude of dining and imbibing options (like refined riverfront seafood–focused Aqua Star Southern Coastal Kitchen), a Heavenly Day Spa, Har-Tru tennis courts, and the Savannah area's only PGA championship golf course.

1 Resort Dr.
912-101-2000, marriott.com

EXPLORE THE MAGIC OF DOLPHINS
RIGHT FROM DOWNTOWN

Downtown-based Dolphin Magic offers one-and-a-half- to two-hour nature and history tours that "guarantee" Atlantic bottlenose dolphin sightings or the next trip is on them. The tours typically head out toward Tybee Island and, in addition to dolphin sightings, include a narrated history of Savannah's waterways, stunning scenery of the rivers, marshes, and barrier islands and possible sights including Fort Jackson, Fort Pulaski, Elba Island, Cockspur Island, the Cockspur Island Lighthouse, Tybee Island Light Station, and more. Running from March to November, the trip route and duration varies, depending on where dolphins are located. The spacious tour boat holds up to 48 passengers, and there is a bathroom onboard. Rain checks are graciously offered, if it does happen to be raining the day of the tour.

313 E River St.
912-897-4990, dolphin-magic.com

BOWL FOR BEER, GREAT FOOD, AND MORE
AT POOLER'S PREMIER BOWL & BISTRO

Offering the best bowling facility and experience within at least 150 miles of Savannah, Premier Bowl & Bistro features much more than just great bowling. With state-of-the-art bowling lanes offered by the hour and by the game, Premier Bowl & Bistro also offers arcade games for all ages, pool tables, and a banquet room. The Bistro features Pooler's largest bar, serving twenty beers on tap and handcrafted cocktails, plus an immensely popular happy hour. The Bistro offers a wide variety of selections that are sure to satisfy any hunger, including wings, tasty burgers, and fresh pizza from their brick oven. They also have daily specials and monthly events, including the Glow Party, Low-Country Boil, themed party nights, and more.

4 Towne Center Ct., Pooler
912-727-4646, poolerbowl.com

HORSE AROUND
AT RED GATE FARMS

Situated less than ten minutes from downtown Savannah, but in another world, Red Gate Farms is located on moss-draped land that once served as encampments for both Union and Confederate soldiers. Today, the farm and campground offers trail rides that showcase the beauty of the nearby countryside just outside Savannah proper. Scheduled in advance and available to those age twelve and older, the thirty- or sixty-minute guided trail rides include instruction (first-timers are welcome!) and all necessary riding equipment (including required helmets). For those non-equestrians, Red Gate Farms also offers smooth carriage rides around the farm featuring the history of Savannah and Red Gate Farms that last about seventy-five minutes.

136 Red Gate Farms Trail
912-239-7855, redgatecampground.com

IMMERSE YOURSELF IN MARINE LIFE
AT THE UGA MARINE EDUCATION CENTER AND AQUARIUM

Located out on Skidaway Island in the Moon River District, just twenty minutes from downtown Savannah, the University of Georgia (UGA) Marine Education Center and Aquarium makes for a great island outing to immerse yourself in Georgia's coastal marine life. As home to the first saltwater aquarium in Georgia (opened in 1972), sixteen different exhibits showcase Georgia's coastal fish, invertebrates, and reptiles. More than two hundred marine animals are featured, as visitors make their way from offshore "live bottom" reefs like Gray's Reef National Marine Sanctuary to inshore tidal creeks. Touch tanks allow visitors to have hands-on interactions with whelks, horseshoe crabs, and more. Along with the aquarium, the facility features a native plant learning garden, shaded picnic areas along the banks of the Skidaway River, and a wheelchair-accessible Jay Wolf Nature Trail and boardwalk.

30 Ocean Science Cir.
912-598-2496, gacoast.uga.edu

TRANSPORT YOURSELF BACK IN TIME
AT THE SAVANNAH-OGEECHEE CANAL

Situated just twenty minutes southwest of downtown, the Historic Savannah–Ogeechee Canal Society Museum & Nature Center transports visitors back to the time when the Savannah–Ogeechee Canal played a vital role in Georgia's economy. Built between 1826 and 1830 by African American and Irish laborers, the 16.5-mile six-lock canal was used to transport crops and goods from inland plantations to the Savannah River and bustling port of Savannah. It operated until the early 1890s, when the Central of Georgia Railroad better served transportation needs. Today, the fascinating destination (open Saturdays and Sundays) includes a museum featuring exhibits on canal history and Georgia flora, fauna, and archaeology, two of the six locks, a half-mile trail on the original towpath, an additional four miles of hiking trails, a butterfly garden, birding and other wildlife watching, and the fun Swamp Store.

681 Fort Argyle Rd.
912-748-8068, savannahogeecheecanal.org

CATCH A WAVE
WITH TYBEE SURF LESSONS

The island setting, beach, sand, and waves of Tybee Island make it a perfect place to go surfing for first-timers and veterans alike, and Tybee Surf Lessons makes it easy to catch a wave. Owned and operated by Savannah native Turner Horton, who has been teaching surfing for more than twenty years and is certified by the National Surf Schools and Instructors Association, varied lessons are available daily and year-round, including private (one to five people) and group (six or more participants) lessons, which are ideal for bachelor and bachelorette parties, and other groups, after-school programs, stand-up paddleboarding, kayaking, and more.

tybeesurflessons.com

EXTRA CREDIT
These dudes even offer ukulele lessons!

COME SAIL AWAY
WITH COMPASS SAILING

Savannah is surrounded by water and a sailing adventure with Compass Sailing provides a great way to explore the area. Captain Steve Horton, who happens to be the father of Turner Horton, owner of Tybee Surf Lessons, provides custom charter yacht excursions out of Bull River Marina aboard a classic thirty-eight-foot Morgan sailing yacht named the Zingara. The marina is ideally situated between Savannah and Tybee Island, just a few miles from Wassaw Sound and the Atlantic Ocean. Sit back, relax, and count the egrets and dolphins, or try the helm under Steve's supervision. Charters last anywhere from four hours to a full day. Soft drinks are provided, but those in the know bring their favorite beverages and picnic supplies to sail away.

912-441-3265
compasssailing.com

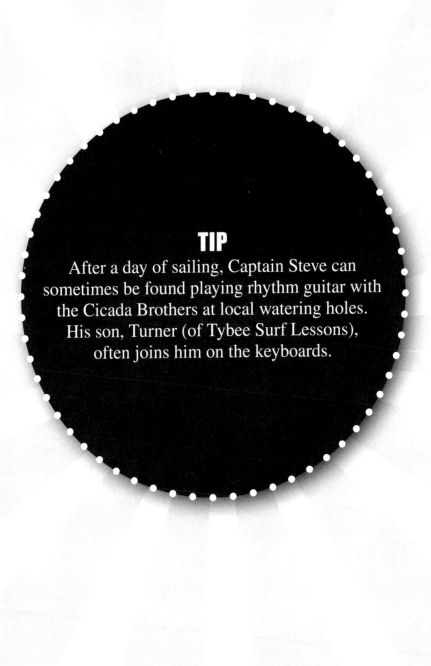

TIP

After a day of sailing, Captain Steve can sometimes be found playing rhythm guitar with the Cicada Brothers at local watering holes. His son, Turner (of Tybee Surf Lessons), often joins him on the keyboards.

DO BAMBOO AND SO MUCH MORE
AT COASTAL GEORGIA BOTANICAL GARDENS AT THE HISTORIC BAMBOO FARM

The Coastal Georgia Botanical Gardens at the Historic Bamboo Farm is a historic public garden located less than fifteen miles from Savannah. The Garden is part of the University of Georgia's College of Agricultural & Environmental Sciences and offers year-round opportunities for visitors to connect with nature and be inspired through beautiful display gardens and collections. The Barbour Lathrop Bamboo Collection boosts more than seventy species of bamboo and dates back to 1919. Other popular collections include the Judge Arthur Solomon Camellia Trail, Stan Gray's Rivers of Iris, Cottage Garden, Formal and White Gardens, Crepe Myrtle Allee, Trustees Garden, Shade and Sun Gardens, and an amazing Orchid Greenhouse. They also offer year-round educational classes and workshops for all ages and abilities, and the popular Camelia Festival in February and December Nights & Holiday Lights.

2 Canebrake Rd.
912-921-5460, coastalbg.uga.edu

TAKE A WALK ON THE WILD SIDE
AT OATLAND ISLAND WILDLIFE CENTER

With more than 175 acres of maritime forest, salt marsh, and freshwater wetlands providing natural habitats for fifty-plus species of indigenous Georgia wildlife, Oatland Island Wildlife Center is an outdoors haven less than five miles east of downtown. Along with two miles of scenic nature trails, possible wildlife sightings, encounters, and exhibits include the wolf pack at the Wolf Wilderness exhibit, birds of prey, bobcats, cougars, alligators, eagles, and more. There's also an outstanding gift shop with lots of "wild" souvenir options after a walk on Savannah's wild side.

711 Sandtown Rd.
912-395-1212, oatlandisland.org

SKID ON OVER
TO SKIDAWAY ISLAND STATE PARK

This 588-acre coastal state park is situated on Skidaway Narrows, which is part of Georgia's Intracoastal Waterway. The Moon River District park features six miles of trails leading through maritime forest and past salt marshes to a boardwalk and observation tower, where visitors can watch for deer, fiddler crabs, raccoons, egrets, and other wildlife. The popular Sandpiper Trail is a one-mile loop that takes explorers over salt flats and tidal creeks, by a 1930s liquor still site, and onto island hammocks. As a stop on the Colonial Coast Birding Trail, the park also provides birdwatchers the opportunity to see and enjoy the beauty of a kaleidoscope of birds. A scenic campground is nestled under live oaks and Spanish moss, and specific-site camping is now allowed at the park, allowing guests to pick the perfect camping spot.

52 Diamond Causeway
912-598-2300, gastateparks.org/skidawayisland

TAKE A DRIVE
AROUND SAVANNAH NATIONAL WILDLIFE REFUGE

The 31,551-acre Savannah National Wildlife is just ten minutes from bustling downtown Savannah, across the Savannah River and South Carolina state line. Established in 1927 as a preserve and breeding ground for native birds, the refuge is home to a wide variety of wildlife, including several threatened and endangered species (like the manatee, the shortnose sturgeon, and the wood stork). It's part of the Atlantic Flyway and attracts thousands of migratory birds, with more than twenty species of ducks and thirty-plus species of warblers having been recorded over the decades. The refuge also contains nesting habitats for bald eagles, purple gallinules, swallow-tailed kits, anhingas, wood ducks, and more. The best way to see the refuge is on the daylight-only year-round 4.5 mile one-way Laurel Hill Wildlife Drive. A stop at the Visitor Center is highly recommended.

694 Beech Hill Ln., Hardeeville, SC
843-784-2468, fws.gov/refuge/savannah

DRIVE A GOLF BALL DOWN A RUNWAY
AT CROSSWINDS GOLF CLUB
(WELL, NOT QUITE)

Situated adjacent to Savannah/Hilton Head International Airport, appropriately named Crosswinds Golf Club is likely the closest a golfer can come to driving a golf ball down a runway. The pretty golf course is situated on one end of the most-used runway at the airport, so most holes are generally underneath the flight path of incoming and outgoing planes of all sorts, including regularly scheduled commercial flights (the airport offers several direct flights beyond the typical Charlotte and Atlanta service), many private jets (Gulfstream designs and develops aircraft near the airport), and fighter jets pursuing "touch and go" practice.

232 James B. Blackburn Dr.
912-966-1909, crosswindsgolfclub.com

TIP

Be sure to ask staff at the golf course or in the award-winning airport about the four graves in the runway. The graves are from the 1800s, and they were left in place after the rest of the original cemetery's graves were moved to Bonaventure Cemetery when they built the airport.

CATCH
A SAVANNAH BANANAS
BASEBALL GAME

The Savannah Bananas college league baseball team plays their games at historic Grainger Stadium every summer. Their "Fans First. Entertain Always." mission focuses on fun for all ages in every way possible, with many special events, giveaways, and more. The Bananas are part of the Coastal Plain League, with fifteen other teams (all from the Carolinas), featuring some of the country's top college players. The Coastal Plain League is considered one of the top prospect leagues for college players with Major League Baseball aspirations. More than 1,200 players from the Coastal Plain League have been drafted, with more than six hundred former players in Minor League Baseball, and more than seventy-five alums having made it to the majors (including Cy Young winner Justin Verlander, Nationals star Ryan Zimmerman, and former Red Sox favorite Kevin Youkilis).

1401 E Victory Dr.
912-712-2482, savannahbananas.com

HIT THE ICE
AT THE SAVANNAH HOCKEY CLASSIC

For two days every January, Savannah hosts four talented college ice hockey teams for four games in downtown's Savannah Civic Center. Officially the Savannah Hockey Classic, the first "Rumble in the Rink" took place in 1999, and it's been a popular weekend to hit the ice ever since. Four top southern hockey teams that currently play in the tournament with the hopes of taking the Thrasher Cup trophy include the University of Georgia, Georgia Tech, University of Florida, and Florida State. Along with the hockey games, other Savannah Hockey Classic highlights include unique merchandise, chuck-a-puck and on ice games.

savannahhockeyclassic.com

EXTRA CREDIT
If you like your icy experiences in a cup anytime of year, head to one of two Wet Willie's locations (20 Jefferson St. at City Market and 101 E River St.), and don't forget about Savannah's "open container" policy. Many Wet Willie's fans from near and far might not know that the company is based in Savannah.
wetwillies.com

GO RETRO
AT THE SAVANNAH SPEED CLASSIC

You don't have to own a vintage vehicle to enjoy the Savannah Speed Classic. Known for history-making events, historic buildings, and more, many don't know that Savannah was also the historic birthplace of Grand Prix auto racing in America. The city hosted the American Grand Prize race in 1908, ran the Grand Prix in 1910, and then hosted the prestigious Vanderbilt Cup in 1911. Taking place on Hutchinson Island, the Savannah Speed Classic features a unique road race experience on the island's classic ten-turn, 1.965-mile Grand Prize of America Road Course. From pre–World War I cars that ran in a Vanderbilt Cup race to classic MGs, Porsches, and Jaguars, the Savannah Speed Classic provides a rolling history of motorsports, including races and in-seat experiences, like "hot lap" rides and touring laps. Pit access is available to anyone with a ticket.

svra.com

EXTRA CREDIT
The Savannah Speed Classic is part of the nine-day "Speedweek" each fall, which includes the Club Car Jamboree, the Motoring Midway, and the Hilton Head Island Concours d'Elegance & Motoring Festival.
hhiconcours.com

PADDLE SAVANNAH

Thanks to its coastal location, including the Atlantic Ocean, many rivers, creeks, and marshlands, the entire Savannah area offers an abundance of paddling opportunities, including kayaking, stand-up paddleboarding, canoeing, and more. From the Savannah River out to Tybee Island and beyond, the possibilities are almost endless. The bucolic scenery, wildlife, and low-country quiet make paddling Savannah a special experience. Various outfitters abound, and it's best to call ahead or visit websites to find the best fit for paddling Savannah your way.

Aqua Dog Kayak Company
912-659-0334, aquadawgkayak.com

North Island Surf & Kayak
912-786-4000, northislandkayak.com

East Coast Paddleboarding
912-484-3200,
eastcoastpaddleboarding.com

Savannah Canoe & Kayak
912-341-9502,
savannahcanoeandkayak.com

Moon River Kayak Tours
912-344-1310, moonriverkayak.com

Sea Kayak Georgia
912-786-8732, seakayakgeorgia.com

Tybee Jet Ski & Watersports
912-786-8062, tybeejetski.com

Wormsloe State Historic Site
Photo courtesy of visitsavannah.com

CULTURE AND HISTORY

"SEE 3"
WITH THE COASTAL HERITAGE SOCIETY

Founded in 1975 to provide educational experiences for the public through the preservation and presentation of historical resources in coastal Georgia and adjacent regions, the Coastal Heritage Society manages six unique museums throughout the Savannah area: Savannah History Museum, Savannah Children's Museum, Georgia State Railroad Museum, Old Fort Jackson, Pin Point Heritage Museum, and the Harper Fowlkes House. Their value-packed "See 3 Pass" for both adults and children (ages two to twelve) is valid for three days, and it can help guests visit a variety of museums at a significant discount. Local visitors can also purchase a membership to enjoy unlimited admission to all six sites year-round.

chsgeorgia.org

SOAK UP SAVANNAH'S HISTORY
AT SAVANNAH HISTORY MUSEUM

Savannah History Museum in Tricentennial Park brings history alive with many interactive exhibits from 1733 and through modern day Savannah. Located in the historic Central of Georgia Railway's Passenger Station, highlights include the bench from *Forrest Gump*, Johnny Mercer's Grammy and Oscar, a 1908 steam locomotive, a cotton gin, a collection of military artifacts, a re-creation of the office of an early Savannah dentist, and much more. Battlefield Memorial Park is adjacent to the museum and stands as a memorial to those who fought in the Battle of Savannah, the second bloodiest battle in the American Revolution. On select scheduled days, guests can participate in a "Loyalists and Liberty" tour, where participants experience a musket firing demonstration, march like soldiers going into battle, and hear about the personalities that shaped Savannah's fight for freedom. There's also the "Last Houses of Frogtown" tour, where participants learn about two of the last three existing nineteenth-century structures that were once part of the historically significant Savannah neighborhood called Frogtown.

303 Martin Luther King Jr. Blvd.
912-651-6825, chsgeorgia.org

BUY
A SAVANNAH TOUR PASS

Locals and visitors who plan to visit a lot of Savannah attractions over a period of one to three consecutive days will want to buy a Savannah Tour Pass. Featuring more than thirty different options, the Savannah Tour Pass typically saves at least 50 percent off separate admission prices. There are more than a dozen "Featured Attractions" that require a reservation (two are included in the one-day pass, three with the two-day pass, and four for the three-day pass). There are an additional twenty-plus "Walk-In Attractions," which require no reservation and can be visited anytime during the duration of the pass. The mobile pass and guide features make the pass extremely easy to use.

843-410-2577

tourpass.com

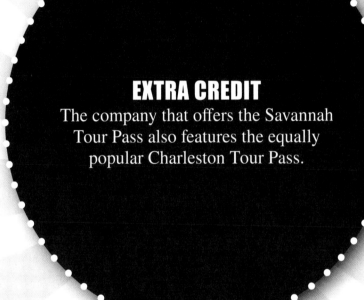

EXTRA CREDIT
The company that offers the Savannah Tour Pass also features the equally popular Charleston Tour Pass.

STROLL THROUGH HISTORY
AT BONAVENTURE CEMETERY

Bonaventure Cemetery, on the banks of the Wilmington River just east of downtown, was founded in 1846, and it became a public cemetery in 1907. Thanks to its tree-lined roads, notable gravesites, including those of singer/songwriter Johnny Mercer, former Georgia Governor Edward Telfair, legendary Savannah child ambassador Gracie Watson, and famed photographer Jack Leigh (who shot the iconic *Midnight in the Garden of Good And Evil* cover), unique cemetery sculpture and architecture, and lots of folklore associated with it, Bonaventure Cemetery was a popular locals and tourist destination long before it was featured in *Midnight in the Garden of Good and Evil*. Interested visitors will want to stop at the helpful Bonaventure Administrative Building at the entrance to the cemetery for a self-guided tour map, mobile tour app information, specific locations of interest, and more.

330 Bonaventure Rd.
912-651-6843, savannahga.gov/864/bonaventure-cemetery

EXTRA CREDIT
There are several Bonaventure Cemetery tour options with local companies, including the Bonaventure Historical Society, Bonaventure Cemetery Tours, and Bonaventure Don, among many others. bonaventurehistorical.org, bonaventurecemeterytours.com, bonaventuredon.com

TIP

Situated right downtown, historic Colonial Park Cemetery is also well worth a visit. It was established around 1750 and was the original burial ground for Christ Parish Church before being enlarged and opened to all denominations later in the century. Many distinguished Savannahians are buried here, including Button Gwinnett, a signer of the Declaration of Independence. Colonial Park Cemetery is also a popular ghost tour stop.

BECOME A PARTNER IN PRESERVATION
WITH A PRESERVATION PASS

It's easy to tour three of Savannah's historic sites where the preservation movement began and that have been named National Historic Landmarks. The Andrew Low House is an 1848 Italianate mansion furnished with period pieces from generations of the Low family and other related families, and a lovely courtyard and historic garden. The Davenport House Museum provides a glimpse of Savannah life in the 1820s in a Federal-style house built by master builder Isaiah Davenport. Finally, Ships of the Sea Maritime Museum is located in the historic William Scarbrough House and highlights Savannah's rich maritime history and the largest private gardens in the Historic District. Purchasing the Preservation Pass currently saves more than twenty dollars, based on separate entry to all three sites, and is available at each museum.

Andrew Low House
329 Abercorn St.
912-233-1828, andrewlowhouse.com

Davenport House Museum
324 E State St.
912-236-8097,
davenporthousemuseum.org

Ships of the Sea Maritime Museum (Scarbrough House)
31 Martin Luther King Jr. Blvd.
912-232-1511, shipsofthesea.org

PAY TRIBUTE
AT THE NATIONAL MUSEUM OF THE MIGHTY EIGHTH AIR FORCE

With a mission statement, "They Saved the World. We Save Their Stories," the National Museum of the Mighty Eighth Air Force is a 90,000-square-foot museum that tells the stories of character, courage, valor, and patriotism of the heroes of the Eighth. Visitors step into the General Lewis E. Lyle Rotunda and are immediately surrounded by history. Lyle flew more than seventy bombing missions in World War II and envisioned the National Museum of the Mighty Eighth Air Force as the repository for the rich and remarkable history of the Mighty Eighth Air Force. This remarkable history comes to life for visitors through encounters with a historic B-17, *City of Savannah*, an immersive "mission" experience, compelling exhibits, and rare objects, photographs, and other planes from World War II. The museum campus includes five static aircraft, the Memorial Gardens, and the Chapel of the Fallen Angels.

175 Bourne Ave., Pooler
912-748-8888, mightyeighth.org

HIT THE RAILS
AT THE GEORGIA STATE RAILROAD MUSEUM

The Georgia State Railroad Museum is a great place to immerse yourself in America's fascinating railroad history and learn about how the expansion of the railroad shaped Savannah and its people. This National Historic Landmark in Tricentennial Park once housed the repair shops and terminal facilities for The Central of Georgia Railway, first chartered in 1833. The museum's main claim to fame is its existing historic railroad structures—the largest collection of antebellum railroad buildings in the United States. The site boasts a working turntable inside the historic Roundhouse, now full of historic railcars and locomotives to explore. Railroad buffs can also experience interactive daily guided tours, including a walk through the Executive Office cars, a ride on the handcar, or a tour of the site from a steam or diesel train. The Model Train Room and play area, known as Locomotion Lab, are also family-friendly favorites.

655 Louisville Rd.
912-651-6823, chsgeorgia.org

GET ARTSY
AT TYBEE COTTAGE ART GALLERY

With an appropriate slogan of "Totally Beachin' Artists," Tybee Island's Tybee Cottage Art Gallery is a great place to view and possibly purchase a wide variety of local art. The small co-op art gallery boasts more than twenty local artists who live on Tybee or in the Savannah area. Genres typically include oils and acrylics, functional and decorative pottery, jewelry, and scented creations like soaps, candles, and teas—in all price ranges. The artists are often on site and available to chat with visitors. They also offer special markets and events throughout the year, including pop-up painting demonstrations.

1209 US Highway 80, Tybee Island
912-675-8824, facebook.com/tybeecottageartgallery

SEE THREE CENTURIES OF HISTORY
AT WORMSLOE STATE HISTORIC SITE

Located on the grounds of the one-time eighteenth-century colonial estate of Noble Jones and just ten miles southeast of downtown in the Moon River District, today's Wormsloe State Historic Site provides the opportunity to see three centuries of history in one place. Jones was a carpenter who arrived in Georgia in 1733 along with James Oglethorpe as part of the first group of area settlers from England. He would serve the colony as a doctor, constable, Royal Councilor, Native American agent, and surveyor before he died at the start of the American Revolution. His descendants maintained the property until the state of Georgia bought most of the estate in 1973. Today, a stunning avenue of live oaks and Spanish moss leads to the former estate, which offers a glimpse into colonial times in coastal Georgia through museum exhibits, nature trails past tabby ruins, and costumed interpreters exhibiting the skills and tools of the period during special events.

7601 Skidaway Rd.
912-353-3023, gastateparks.org/wormsloe

TIP

There is also a small museum and a short film about the site and the founding of Georgia and a gift shop featuring all things Peach State.

GO GULLAH/GEECHEE
AT PIN POINT HERITAGE MUSEUM

Situated just south of downtown on the banks of the Moon River, the Pin Point community was founded after the Civil War in the 1890s by freedmen (many from coastal Georgia's Sea Islands). In this Moon River District historic setting, formerly enslaved people and their descendants were first able to purchase their own land and build a community. The Gullah/Geechee culture, language, religion, foodways, and stories have remained strong for decades because of the community's relative isolation. Today, Pin Point Heritage Museum pays tribute to the community through a variety of exhibits, multimedia presentations, and waterfront views that haven't changed in centuries. The museum is located in the buildings of the former A. S. Varn & Son Oyster and Crab Factory, which employed many Pin Point residents until its closure in 1985. Be sure to ask about the annual Art & Oysters festival.

9924 Pin Point Ave.
912-355-0064, chsgeorgia.org

BECOME A FAN
OF FLANNERY O'CONNOR

Renowned writer Flannery O'Connor spent the first thirteen years of her life (1925–1938) in Savannah, and her childhood home on Lafayette Square welcomes visitors. O'Connor wrote more than 30 short stories, including "A Good Man Is Hard to Find" and "Good Country People," as well as several acclaimed novels, including *The Violent Bear It Away* and *Wise Blood,* which was later adapted for the silver screen by director John Huston. The Flannery O'Connor Childhood Home has been restored, and it reflects life during the Depression. It includes the Bruckheimer Library, which features children's books from young O'Connor's personal collection, several exhibits, and the house's original backyard, where O'Connor is purported to have taught a chicken to walk backwards.

207 E Charlton St.
912-233-6014, flanneryoconnorhome.org

TIP
The gift shop features a collection of books by and about O'Connor and other gift items for new or longtime O'Connor fans.

EXPLORE SAVANNAH'S AFRICAN AMERICAN CULTURE
AT THE BEACH INSTITUTE AND BEYOND

Founded in 1867 during Reconstruction as the first official school for Savannah's African Americans, The Beach Institute's original building is now home to The Beach Institute African-American Cultural Center. Located downtown, today's Center features several museum galleries, a historic classroom, a documentary screening room, a popular genealogy research facility, the Ulysses Davis Woodworking Collection, and an award-winning garden ideal for reflection. The Beach Institute's offerings also include the historic restored 1896 King-Tisdell Cottage, which was the Victorian-style home of Sarah King and Robert Tisdell, members of Savannah's vibrant African American entrepreneurial class at the turn of the century. It's nearby, at 514 E Huntingdon St., and admission is included with a ticket for The Beach Institute.

502 Harris St.
912-355-8868, beachinstitute.org

EXTRA CREDIT: THERE ARE MANY OTHER WAYS TO EXPLORE SAVANNAH'S RICH AFRICAN AMERICAN HISTORY AND CULTURE.

Vaughnette Goode-Walker's Footprints of Savannah Walking Tours
footprintsofsavannah.com

Johnnie Brown's Freedom Trail Tour
912-398-2785

Ralph Mark Gilbert Civil Rights Museum
460 Martin Luther King Jr. Blvd.
912-777-6099

EXPLORE TWO HUNDRED YEARS OF ART, HISTORY, AND ARCHITECTURE
AT THE TELFAIR MUSEUMS

With three unique museums for one ticket price, downtown's Telfair Museums offer a great way to experience two hundred years of Savannah's art, history, and architecture. The Telfair Academy on Telfair Square is a former mansion built during 1818–1819 for Alexander Telfair, son of Revolutionary War patriot and Georgia governor Edward Telfair. Highlights of a visit include the entrance hall, the octagonal reception room, the dining room, the drawing room, the original kitchen, and two huge art galleries in a nineteenth-century addition. Nearby and also on Telfair Square, the Jepson Center awaits with a modern Moshe Safdie–designed building that houses a world-renowned art collection of the works of notable American artists and temporary exhibits. The Jepson Center's Gift Shop is well worth a stop. Five blocks away, the Owens-Thomas House & Slave Quarters features one of the earliest intact urban slave quarters in the South, a parterre-style garden, interactive exhibits, and many decorative arts and furnishings.

Telfair Academy	**Jepson Center**	**Owens-Thomas House**
121 Barnard St.	207 W York St.	**& Slave Quarters**
912-790-8800	912-790-8800	124 Abercorn St.
		912-790-8800

telfair.org

TIP

Don't miss the original *Bird Girl*
sculpture from *Midnight in the Garden of Good
and Evil* fame in the upstairs gallery
of the Telfair Academy.

EXPERIENCE
THE FALL OF FORT PULASKI

Fort Pulaski National Monument not only preserves the fort's nineteenth-century story, but it protects nearly 5,000 acres of coastal Georgia wetlands. Deemed indestructible thanks to its location and unique design, Fort Pulaski's fall during the American Civil War can be relived on Cockspur Island. Accessible by bridge just fourteen miles east of downtown, just before Tybee Island (where Union forces set up their many cannons for the bombardment), today's preserved Fort Pulaski includes many of the original features that made the fort one of the strongest along the Atlantic coast. The park also features several interesting trails and a marsh ecosystem that supports numerous acres of coastal wetlands and a multitude of plant life and wildlife that make Fort Pulaski National Monument the perfect escape for every historian and naturalist.

101 Fort Pulaski Rd.
912-786-5787, nps.gov/fortpulaski

GET HIP
TO CONTEMPORARY ART
AT SCAD MUSEUM OF ART

Leave it to the hip creatives at the Savannah College of Art and Design (SCAD) to provide a haven for contemporary art and innovative voices at the SCAD Museum of Art. The museum is a renowned contemporary art destination that features established and emerging international artists through rotating exhibitions and commissioned work. In addition to the ongoing exhibitions, the SCAD Museum of Art has permanent collections including the Walter O. Evans Collection of African American Art, the Modern and Contemporary Art Collection, the Earle W. Newton Collection of British and American Art, The Nineteenth- and Twentieth-Century Photography Collection, and the SCAD Costume Collection. The collections are regularly used in the beautiful museum lobby and as part of the rotating exhibitions.

601 Turner Blvd.
912-525-7191, scadmoa.org

EXTRA CREDIT
The museum hosts the annual deFINE Art festival in late February, which consists of special commissions, exhibitions, lectures, and performances for SCAD students, alumni, and the local community.

WORSHIP THE HISTORY
OF THE FIRST AFRICAN
BAPTIST CHURCH

The First African Baptist Church is not only considered the oldest African American congregation in the United States, being founded in 1773, it also stands as a symbol of African American history. The church served as a safe house for slaves and was a stop along the Underground Railroad. The pews in the balcony—original to the 1859 sanctuary— were built by slaves, and visitors can still see markings of the African dialect. They can also see the subfloor below the lower auditorium that was part of the Underground Railroad. The light fixtures, baptismal pool, and pipe organ are also original to the church. Tours are available Tuesday through Saturday at 11:00 a.m., 2:00 p.m., and 4:00 p.m. and on Sunday at 1:00 p.m.

23 Montgomery St.
912-233-6597, firstafricanbc.com

TIP
Look for the holes in the sanctuary floor, which create a design meant to look like a tribal symbol. They served as air holes for escaped slaves who came through the Underground Railroad and runaway slaves during the Civil War.

THE CITY IS FILLED WITH OTHER HISTORICALLY SIGNIFICANT CHURCHES AND PLACES OF WORSHIP.

Cathedral of St. John the Baptist
222 E Harris St.
912-233-4709,
savannahcathedral.org

St. John's Episcopal Church
325 Bull St.
912-232-1251,
stjohnssav.org

Christ Church
28 Bull St.
912-236-2500,
christchurchsavannah.org

Temple Mickve Israel
20 E Gordon St.
912-233-1547,
mickveisrael.org

Independent Presbyterian Church
207 Bull St.
912-236-3346,
ipcsav.org

Trinity United Methodist Church
225 W President St.
912-233-4766,
trinity1848.org

Lutheran Church of the Ascension
120 Bull St.
912-232-4151,
ascensionsavannah.org

Unitarian Universalist Church
311 E Harris St.
912-549-0326,
uusavannah.org

KID AROUND
AT THE SAVANNAH CHILDREN'S MUSEUM

Great for kids and kids at heart, Savannah Children's Museum is an entirely outdoor educational space located in the former Central of Georgia Railway's carpentry shop in Tricentennial Park. There are currently more than a dozen different interactive and hands-on exhibits for children ages two to ten, including an exploration maze, a reading nook, sensory garden, and much more. Each exhibit has been carefully designed to incorporate Georgia educational standards and developmentally appropriate, stimulating, and challenging experiences that encourage children to learn through play.

655 Louisville Rd.
912-651-4292, chsgeorgia.org

SEE THE LIGHT
AT TYBEE LIGHTHOUSE & MUSEUM

Officially called the "Tybee Island Light Station," the Tybee Lighthouse is Georgia's oldest and tallest and welcomes visitors every day, except Tuesday. Originally ordered by General James Oglethorpe, governor of the thirteenth colony back in 1732, the Tybee lighthouse has been providing mariners with a safe entrance into the Savannah River from the Atlantic Ocean ever since. Today, the 178 steps along a circular stairway to the top offers platforms for resting and windows for viewing about every twenty-five steps and the view from the top is well worth the effort. Two lighthouse keeper cottages and the summer kitchen are also available to tour, as is the Tybee Island Museum housed in the Fort Screven Battery Garland across the street.

30 Meddin Dr., Tybee Island
912-786-5801, tybeelighthouse.org

SEE SAVANNAH
IN THE MOVIES

Savannah's charming locations have served film directors well in many movies. Those who want to explore *Midnight in the Garden of Good and Evil* will want to visit the Mercer-Williams House and see the original famed *Bird Girl* sculpture at the Telfair Academy. If *Forrest Gump* is more your style, you'll likely want to see the park bench in Chippewa Square, where Tom Hanks waxed poetically as to why "life is like a box of chocolates." The bench is no longer on the square, but you can visit it at the Savannah History Museum. The film's beloved Jenny worked as a waitress at Debi's Restaurant, just off of Wright Square. The Six Pence Pub on Bull Street is where the nightgown-clad Julia Roberts argues with her husband, Dennis Quaid, in *Something to Talk About*. Further afield, the Tybee Island Wedding Chapel played a role in Nicholas Sparks's *The Last Song*, while *Magic Mike XXL* featured Tybee's kitschy Dunes Inn & Suites.

Mercer-Williams House
429 Bull St.
912-236-6352, mercerhouse.com

Telfair Academy
121 Barnard St.
912-790-8800, telfair.org

Savannah History Museum
303 Martin Luther King Jr. Blvd.
912-651-6825, chsgeorgia.org

Debi's Restaurant
10 W State St.
912-236-3322, debisrestaurant.com

Six Pence Pub
235 Bull St.
912-233-3151, sixpencepub.com

Tybee Island Wedding Chapel
1114 1st St, Tybee Island
912-786-9099, tybeeweddingchapel.com

Dunes Inn & Suites
1409 Butler Ave., Tybee Island
912-786-4591, dunesinn.com

GET FIRED UP
AT OLD FORT JACKSON

Strategically situated three miles east of downtown on the Savannah River, Old Fort Jackson was originally built in 1808 to guard entry by ships coming up the river. It remains Georgia's oldest standing brick fort and one of the East Coast's oldest brick fortifications. Constructed on an older earthen battery from the Revolutionary War and named for Georgia patriot James Jackson, Fort Jackson was garrisoned by soldiers during the War of 1812 and again during the Civil War, first by Confederate militia and then by Federal troops after General William Tecumseh Sherman's "March to the Sea." Today, it's easy to get fired up at Old Fort Jackson, thanks to daily cannon firings and interactive demonstrations that have brought new life to Georgia's oldest brick fortification.

1 Fort Jackson Rd.
912-232-3945, chsgeorgia.org

HEAD TO
HENRY FORD'S SOUTHERN TOWN OF RICHMOND HILL

Located on the banks of the Great Ogeechee River, twenty miles southwest of downtown Savannah, quaint Richmond Hill is known as "Henry Ford's Southern Town" because the automotive industrialist made the area his winter home for almost twenty-five years. The Richmond Hill History Museum is a great place to learn about Ford's time in town and the history of the town in general (there's also a great gift shop). The museum is in the former Ford kindergarten building, whereas the helpful Richmond Hill Convention and Visitors Bureau is in the old Ford bakery. Other Richmond Hill area must-do possibilities include the Coastal Bryan Heritage Trail (featuring more history and the area's scenic beauty), Civil War–era Fort McAllister State Park, varied accommodations options for overnights, and several tasty restaurants such as waterfront Marker 107 and Fish Tales, Melody's Coastal Café & Sand Bar Cantina, the classic Southern buffet at Bubba's Bistro, and Smokin Pig, "The Bar-B-Q Joint."

10750 Ford Ave. (Richmond Hill Convention and Visitors Bureau),
Richmond Hill
912-756-2676, visitrichmondhill.com

EXTRA CREDIT
Known as "Savannah's Front Porch," Port Wentworth makes for another fun outing, including lots of historical and natural pursuits.
visitportwentworth.com

GO GIRL SCOUTING
AT THE JULIETTE GORDON
LOW BIRTHPLACE

Savannah native Juliette Gordon Low was a daughter, debutante, wife, adventurer, and artist who went on to form the original Girl Scouts organization in 1912, after meeting Boy Scouts founder Robert Baden-Powell. What started with eighteen Savannah girls eventually grew into an international organization serving millions. Low's birthplace was Savannah's first National Historic Landmark, and it remains one of the city's most popular places to visit, with its original and period furnishings adorning seven spacious rooms, elaborately carved millwork, decorative plaster ceilings, and a stunning staircase with a curved mahogany rail. Numerous works of art, including many pieces created by Low herself, are on display throughout the house. There's also a quiet urban courtyard and garden and a gift shop featuring local gifts, items made by women and girls around the globe, and Girl Scouts merchandise.

10 E Oglethorpe Ave.
912-233-4501, juliettegordonlowbirthplace.org

TIP
Girl Scouts members receive a discount on admission.

TAKE A TROLLEY TOUR
AND MORE WITH OLD SAVANNAH TOURS

Offering Savannah tours since 1979, locally owned Old Savannah Tours features a wide variety of tour options to suit all interests and times available. Their most popular tour, "On & Off," provides a perfect introduction to Savannah and a great way to move between sights, restaurants, and other downtown attractions. The all-day ticket on open trolleys features sixteen convenient stops. There's also the one-hundred-minute narrated overview tour on open trolleys, which includes historic reenactors (think Forrest Gump, Juliette Gordon Low, and many others). Other options include the "Savannah Experience" tour (a three-hour tour in a climate-controlled mini-bus), "Grave Encounters Telfair Ghost Tour," "BOO Y'ALL Comedy Ghost Tour," and a "Savannah Riverboat Sightseeing Tour." Be sure to ask about combination and package tickets for savings on many of their tours.

912-234-8128 or 800-517-9007, oldsavannahtours.com

EXTRA CREDIT
Of course, a tourist town like Savannah has many other companies offering varied touring options, including Old Town Trolley Tours, which also offers tours in many other popular destinations in America. trolleytours.com

HIT THE HEARSE
FOR A GHOST TOUR

An authentic and previously used hearse has to be the most appropriate vehicle for ghost tours and Savannah's famed Hearse Ghost Tours carts "victims" on nightly outings. The seventy-five- to ninety-minute tours introduce hearse passengers to Savannah's famous haunts in the Historic and Victorian districts, along with ghost stories and paranormal activities as they sit in comfortable raised chairs in the open-air rear of the reconfigured hearse. There are several convenient downtown pickup locations, and the hearse has room for eight bodies, dead or alive (there's discounted pricing for kids ten and under, while dead passengers ride for free).

912-695-1578
hearseghosttours.com

TIP
Ask your driver to take you to the one-time butcher shop where the owner killed his family and then hung himself. There's now a small oddity museum, including a shrunken head, haunted dolls, a three-headed duck, and much more.

HEAD "HOME"
TO THE HARPER FOWLKES HOUSE

Overlooking serene Orleans Square, Harper Fowlkes House was built in 1842 in the Greek Revival style. Entrepreneur Alida Harper Fowlkes purchased the home at a tax sale in 1939 and donated the house to the Society of the Cincinnati in the State of Georgia in 1985. She wanted the house to showcase the lifestyle of the mid-1800s and stipulated that her furnishings would remain with the home. The Harper Fowlkes House opened in 2008 as a museum to share the vision and mission Alida saw for the future of the home. Today, guests of the home can take hourly tours and learn about the richly furnished interiors, important oil portraits, and original architectural details of the historic house.

230 Barnard St.
912-234-2180, chsgeorgia.org

SHOPPING AND FASHION

BOOK IT
TO A BOOKSTORE

Whether it's the latest beach read, a Savannah-focused cookbook (think Paula Deen's offerings and many more), or a book about the city's fascinating history, Savannah is a town of readers. E. Shaver, Bookseller, was founded by Ed and Esther Shaver back in 1975, and it has grown into a favorite destination for readers near and far. Currently owned and operated since 2015 by longtime employee Jessica Osborne, E. Shaver is better than ever. Situated just off Madison Square in a historic 1842 building, the bustling bookstore includes several rooms of varied books, reading-oriented gift items, lots of events and signings, several fluffy bookstore cats, and the Savannah Tea Room, which is a great place to enjoy a newly purchased book over a cup of tea (no coffee in this tea-focused haven; they also sell tasty cookies that pair well with tea and other tea paraphernalia).

326 Bull St.
912-234-7257, eshaverbooks.com, savannahtearoom.com

EXTRA CREDIT

Also located in the heart of the Historic District (at 6 E Liberty St.) is The Book Lady, another beloved bookstore with a story (and more than forty genres of both new and gently used titles, rare first editions, and out-of-print books). The inimitable Anita Raskin opened the bookshop in 1978. After Raskin passed away in 2002, Joni Saxon-Giusti—who worked at The Book Lady for many years—purchased and revamped the business and has overseen its phenomenal growth and relocation.
thebookladybookstore.com

OTHER AREA BOOKSTORES

Barnes & Noble Booksellers
7804 Abercorn Ext. #72 (Oglethorpe Mall)
912-353-7757, barnesandnoble.com

Books on Bay
224 W Bay St.
912-236-7115, booksonbay.com

Ex Libris Bookstore
228 Martin Luther King Jr. Blvd.
912-525-7550, scadbookstore.com

TIP:
February's Savannah Book Festival has grown
into a popular annual event for book lovers
(and authors) of all sorts.
savannahbookfestival.org

GET THE ULTIMATE SAVANNAH KEEPSAKE
AT shopSCAD

The unique Savannah College of Art and Design (SCAD) retail gallery, shopSCAD, is a reflection of the city's iconic university and its students, alumni, and faculty members. Located in SCAD's historic Poetter Hall, shopSCAD has been a favorite for both locals and visitors for window shopping and collecting fine art for more than a decade, with a second shop that opened at the university's location in Lacoste, France, in 2014. The talented community of SCAD artists featured in the ever-changing collection have seen their work in renowned galleries, worn by celebrities on red carpets, featured in premier fashion magazines, and in homes around the world. Quite simply, it's a one-stop shop for the ultimate Savannah keepsake. And SCAD's Gryphon tea room is just across the street.

340 Bull St.
912-525-5180, shopscad.com

EXTRA CREDIT
Situated adjacent to shopSCAD in Poetter Hall at 340 Bull St., scadSTORY is an immersive 360-degree journey highlighting the university's more than forty years of life as the most comprehensive art and design school in the world. It's free and open to the public, but reservations are required online.
scadstory.com

GET A COOKIE (OR THREE)
AT BYRD COOKIE COMPANY

With six Savannah-area locations from which to choose (as well as several more in South Carolina and Tennessee), you don't have to look far for your next cookie fix at beloved Byrd Cookie Company. Founded in Savannah in 1924, Byrd Cookie Company is now one of the nation's largest and fastest-growing independent cookie, snack, and gift companies. Known for their "mini cookies—mighty flavor," Byrd bakes a wide variety of delicious cookies, ensuring that there's something for everybody. The original Scotch Oatmeal, the best-selling Key Lime Cooler, regional favorite Georgia Peach Cookie, and the savory Cheddar Pecan Biscuit are just a few of the many flavors available at each Byrd Cookie Company location. If you're not sure what your favorite cookie might be, make the Cookie Bar your first stop for a full sampling of Byrd cookies. Tasty tours of the bakery are available by appointment at the Bakery and Flagship Store.

6700 Waters Ave. (Bakery and Flagship Store), 912-355-1716
213 W St. Julian St. (City Market), 912-721-1563
423 E River St. (River Street), 912-721-1566
300 W River St., Unite #6A (River Street), 912-355-1716
9 Mill Creek Cir., A-2, Pooler, 912-721-1560
200 Tanger Outlets Blvd., Ste. 372, Pooler, 912-721-1549
byrdcookiecompany.com

FUN FACT
Byrd Cookie Company installed a huge 170-foot oven in 2018 to increase their annual production to more than a billion cookies!

SEE WHAT ALL THE BUZZ IS ABOUT
AT SAVANNAH BEE COMPANY

Founded by passionate beekeeper, Ted Dennard, Savannah Bee Company is dedicated to sharing the wonders of honeybees and providing education about the important role they play as pollinators. Each store offers an opportunity to celebrate honeybees in different ways, with honey and mead tastings and a vast selection of honeybee gifts, including specialty honey and beehive-inspired body care products. For an especially memorable and interactive experience, those in the know head to their Wilmington Island Showroom location for a Bee Garden Tour that gives visitors the opportunity to view an observational beehive and get up close and personal with working hives in the garden. Other retail locations across the country include St. Simons Island, Georgia; Atlanta, Georgia; Charleston, South Carolina; Myrtle Beach, South Carolina (Broadway at the Beach and Barefoot Landing); Lake Buena Vista, Florida; Westport, Connecticut; Gatlinburg, Tennessee; Pigeon Forge, Tennessee; Boulder, Colorado; Sedona, Arizona; and counting.

1 W River St., 912-234-7088
104 W Broughton St., 912-233-7875
211 Johnny Mercer Blvd., (Wilmington Island Showroom and Bee Garden Tours), 912-629-0908
savannahbee.com

GO SHOPPING
AT SANDERS GIFTS & HOME ACCENTS

Originally opened as Sanders Country Store back in 1984 and still featuring a country store feel, Sanders Gifts & Home Accents provides one-stop shopping for that special gift, souvenir, or perfect home accent. Situated on Wilmington Island on the way to Tybee Island, on Old Tybee Road, the lavender-and-white gingerbread home-style store is located on the grounds of the Old Mayer Plantation. Highlights of a visit here have to include all the lighted villages upon first entering the store, lots of scented candles, silk flowers, stained glass lamps, a wide array of Savannah keepsakes, Tybee lighthouses, plates, magnets, a huge wall of seashells, and their own line of jams, jellies, and preserves (with samples happily provided before purchase).

7908 US 80
912-897-4861, sandersgiftsandhome.com

FIND THE PERFECT SHOP AND SO MUCH MORE
IN THE STARLAND DISTRICT

Situated just south of downtown proper, Savannah's eclectic Starland District is a great place to head for many unique restaurants, cafés, and the multitude of shops that seemingly have something for everyone. The area has become known as a haven for creative "makers" and entrepreneurs of all sorts, making it ideal for a fun Savannah shopping excursion. The options, among many, include Starlandia Art Supply (trust us, it's so much more than an art supply store), Gypsy World (vintage clothing), Graveface Records & Curiosities (new and used records, plus much more), Sulfur Studios (old office spaces reclaimed as more than two dozen artist studios and a gallery), outdoors- and maker-oriented Superbloom (ask about their unique bicycle wrap skirts), perfectly named Picker Joe's Antique Mall & Vintage Market, the design-focused Emily McCarthy shop, Epiphany Bead and Jewelry Studio, unique gifts and lots more at The Cottage Shop, and many other shopping options (just start strolling Starland).

Starlandia Art Supply
2438 Bull St.
912-417-4561, starlandiasupply.com

Gypsy World
2405 Bull St.
912-335-2620, gypsyworldsavannah.com

Graveface
5 W 40th St.
912-335-8018, graveface.com

Sulfur Studios
2301 Bull St.
912-231-7105, sulfurstudios.org

Superbloom
2418-20 Desoto Ave., forestandfin.com

Picker Joe's Antique Mall & Vintage Market
217-A E 41st St.
912-239-4657, pickerjoes.com

Emily McCarthy
2428 Abercorn St.
912-495-5386, emilymccarthy.com

Epiphany Bead and Jewelry Studio
104 E 41st St.
912-477-3983, epiphany.indiemade.com

The Cottage Shop
2422 Abercorn St.
912-233-3820, thecottageshop.bridgecatalog.com

GET BEACHY
AT SEASIDE SISTERS

Known as Tybee Island's "shore thing," thanks to their coastal cottage style, Seaside Sisters was conceived by a triad of women who love home décor, coastal art, and creative gifts. They specialize in local art, American-made crafts, decorative items, funky furnishings, beautiful baubles, linens, candles, seasonal items, antiques, and women's accessories. They also feature personal finds from famed author Mary Kay Andrews, who is a part-time Tybee Island resident. If you are looking to be inspired, fixing up a house at the seashore, searching for the perfect gift, or simply window shopping, Seaside Sisters will have exactly what you are looking for and will lift your spirits at the same time.

1207 Highway 80 E (North End Market Place), Tybee Island
912-786-9216, seasidesisterstybee.com

TIP
Check out sister company Sweetie Pie (in a little vintage trailer next to Seaside Sisters) for gelato, ice cream, shakes, smoothies, candy, and other sweet treats. Also check out Seaside Sweets (18B Tybrisa St., Tybee Island) for ice cream, gelato, and more.
seasidesisterstybee.com/seaside-sweets

EXTRA CREDIT

Prolific and award-winning author Mary Kay Andrews, who lives in Atlanta full-time, loves Tybee Island so much that she often vacations there. She even has two rental homes listed with Tybee Vacation Rentals. Breeze Inn is a pet-friendly, eclectic, 1943 remodeled cottage that's filled with some of her favorite furniture and other treasures. Ebbtide is a 1932 beach cottage that Andrews restored. It features original touches like board and batten wood paneling, wood ceilings, and beautiful hardwood floors. Of course, Tybee Vacation Rentals has a wide range of other rental possibilities. Although any Andrews novel would be great to read while on Tybee Island, *Savannah Blues*, the sequel *Savannah Breeze*, and *Sunset Beach* seem particularly appropriate beach reads.

tybeevacationrentals.com, marykayandrews.com

GO MARKETING FOR FRESH FOOD AND MORE
AT FORSYTH FARMERS' MARKET

Open every Saturday from 9 a.m. to 1 p.m. on the south end of Forsyth Park, Forsyth Farmers' Market is thriving, with a "producers-only" policy—which means that all vendors have to produce at least 75 percent of the products they sell, with only food and plant vendors invited to sell their wares at the market. The market's list of whole foods vendors typically numbers more than thirty and includes fresh produce, pastured meats, local honey, artisan cheeses, craft breads, baked goods, prepared foods, and of course changes seasonally. The folks at Forsyth Farmers' Market also operate Food Truck 912 (farmtruck912.org), which is a unique mobile farmers market that brings the farmer to people throughout the Savannah area.

Forsyth Park, 803-942-5119
forsythfarmersmarket.com

TIP
Look for sustainably raised fillets of tilapia and aquaponically grown produce from Billy's Botanicals, one of many popular and regular vendors at Forsyth Farmers' Market.

TOWEL OFF
WITH A WEEZIE TOWEL

Savannah-based Weezie has become world-renowned for their lush direct-to-consumer bath towels and other luxurious linens, such as popular bath robes, beach towels, bags, and more. Founders Liz Eichholz and Lindsey Johnson started Weezie after discovering their mutual love of fabrics, and especially lush, plush towels. Luxurious linens have a long lineage in Savannah and throughout the South, where being a great hostess includes providing classic linens to guests. Savannah is known as the Hostess City, after all. Weezie offers a variety of colors and patterns, as well as monogramming and gift cards, all of which is easily accomplished online.

weezietowels.com

TIP
The Weezie "Starter Pack" includes four super-plush towels and two hand towels at a discount, and it makes for a perfect gift. You can also opt for the discounted "Beach Bundle," which includes four beach towels.

GET CORKED
AT CORKHOUSE

Situated in Factor's Walk off Bay Street in a former 1785 grain warehouse, CorkHouse is the United States outpost for Canadian-based Jelinek Cork, which has Eastern European roots dating to 1855. The unique showroom and store specializes in cork and sustainable home décor products, making it a great place to shop for anything from a complete home renovation to a unique Savannah gift. With everything from cork flooring and wall coverings to furniture (think cork stools and chairs), home décor (planters, placemats, soap dishes), hobbies (yoga mats and arts & crafts supplies), cork fashion accessories, wallets and purses, and even shoes, CorkHouse makes it easy to get corked in Savannah.

230 W Bay St.
912-677-3212, corkhouse.com

TIP

You can be the life of the party with personalized wine corks, coasters, or cork place card holders, because CorkHouse can imprint a monogram, logo, or personal message on a variety of products for parties, weddings, corporate events, and more.

Old Town Trolley Tours in front of the
Cathedral of St. John the Baptist
Photo courtesy of visitsavannah.com

SUGGESTED
ITINERARIES

GET OUTSIDE

TOURS AND MORE

THE WILD SIDE

DRINK IT IN

FAMILY AFFAIR

• •

HISTORY LESSONS

SPECTATOR SPORTS

TAKE IN THE ARTS

UNIQUELY SAVANNAH

• •

TASTES OF SAVANNAH

AROUND THE WORLD

St. Patrick's Day Parade
Photo courtesy of visitsavannah.com

ACTIVITIES
BY SEASON

SPRING

Stroll Through History at Bonaventure Cemetery, 88

Tune Into the Savannah Music Festival, 44

Take a Riverboat Cruise on the Savannah River, 61

Go Green on St. Patrick's Day in Savannah, 48

SUMMER

Catch a Savannah Bananas Baseball Game, 78

Eat Where the Elite Eat in their Bare Feet at The Original Crab Shack, 16

Towel Off with a Weezie Towel, 129

Catch a Wave with Tybee Surf Lessons, 68

Get Lucky at Leopold's Ice Cream, 17

Come Sail Away with Compass Sailing, 70

Go Marketing for Fresh Food and More at Forsyth Farmers' Market, 128

FALL

Jam at the Savannah Jazz Festival, 51

See What All the Buzz is About at Savannah Bee Company, 122

Go Retro at the Savannah Speed Classic, 80

Paddle Savannah, 81

Take a Drive Around Savannah National Wildlife Refuge, 75

• •

WINTER

• •

INDEX

• •

• •

144